RESUMES! RESUMES! RESUMES!

2nd Edition

By

Career Press editors

CAREER PRESS
180 Fifth Avenue
P.O. Box 34
Hawthorne, NJ 07507
1-800-CAREER-1
201-427-0229 (outside U.S.)
FAX: 201-427-2037

RESUMES! RESUMES! RESUMES!

2ND EDITION

ISBN 1-56414-159-4, $9.99

Cover design by Digital Perspectives

Contributing editors: Tony Rutigliano, John Sherman and Ellen Scher

Printed in the U.S.A. by Book-mart Press

To order this title by mail, please include price as noted above, $2.50 handling per order, and $1.00 for each book ordered. Send to: Career Press, Inc., 180 Fifth Ave., P.O. Box 34, Hawthorne, NJ 07507.

Or call toll-free 1-800-CAREER-1 (Canada: 201-427-0229) to order using VISA or MasterCard, or for further information on books from Career Press.

Library of Congress Cataloging-in-Publication Data

Resumes! resumes! resumes! / by Career Press editors. -- 2nd ed.
p. cm.
Includes index.
ISBN 1-56414-159-4 : $9.99
1. Résumés (Employment) I. Career Press Inc.
HF5383.R4715 1995
808'.06665--dc20 94-44540
CIP

Contents

Preface

Show me!

Even those of us not from Missouri, the "Show Me" state, live by this motto, particularly when we are learning something new or investigating how we can improve upon skills we might already have.

We learn far more quickly when *shown* how to do something rather than when simply *told* how to do it.

Think about how you might try to tell someone to perform a task as simple as folding a napkin or throwing a ball if you could use words alone. It's a daunting prospect, isn't it? How much tougher that job is when the task is something as vague as resume writing!

Sure, we can fill hundreds of pages delivering good, solid advice on how you can put together the best resume for the job you're going after. And, after reading through the advice, you'd probably be able to compose a fairly solid picture of your experience, education and skills.

But one good resume—a mere 250 or so words—can speak volumes.

In this book, we're going to do even better than show you one good resume. We're going to show you *42* great resumes! We are giving you the best resumes seen by some of the leading recruiting and career counseling professionals in the country, and we're going to explain why they work.

If, as the old saw goes, a picture speaks a thousand words, then these resumes, selected by the likes of Robert Half, founder of Robert Half International, and top executives at companies such as Drake Beam Morin, Inc., Lee Hecht Harrison and Right Associates, will speak volumes.

These are resumes that have helped people land jobs. They are resumes that were remembered—in some cases years after they were originally seen—by recruitment professionals who've seen thousands of such documents.

This book, because it is filled with what works, will *show you* the very best way to write a winning resume.

Introduction

The Best Resumes We've Ever Seen

We found it very interesting at our company that, as we put the first edition of this book together, we were in the midst of searching for someone who could fill an editorial assistant position. Our ad in *The New York Times* classified section drew more than 300 responses in a week! And, busy people all, we had to cull from this stack a short list of candidates in whom we thought we should invest the time to conduct screening interviews.

So, as good-hearted people who deliver job-hunting advice, we pored over every word of every resume, no matter how sloppily typed, and despite the absence of cover letters.

Are you kidding? We did what any average, red-blooded American employer would do. We gave each resume 20 seconds to tell us one of two things: *Read on* or *toss it*.

What is it that determines this magical make or break? As professionals in the subtleties of the job market, we can definitively say, "That depends."

Perhaps it's because the resume is a seventh-generation photocopy. Or maybe it simply renders a portrait that's fuzzy at the edges, and we expect the candidate attached to that resume to be the same way. Or maybe it's that the candidate sent the resume in an envelope that obviously came through the storage room at his or her company and, what's more, sent it through the employer's postage machine.

It might have been that we found a typo in the very first line of the cover letter (while we were still smarting about our name being misspelled).

Eureka!

Just what is it, then, that sets the successful resumes apart? Well, in the case of the search mentioned here, we selected five (that's right *five* candidates from the more than 300 resumes that came to our offices) to interview. Looking back at them, we can make the following generalizations:

- These resumes were neat. All of them were printed on good stock (not photocopy paper); they were laser-printed or typeset; and they were laid out on the page clearly and attractively.

- They were succinct. Notice we didn't say, "short." Such a resume talks about the candidate and his or her accomplishments with clear, concise and precise language.
- They made us feel confident. In the case of this screening process, confident that we would not waste our too-precious time finding out a little bit more about these fabulous five.
- The five successful resumes demonstrated that the candidates had the right educations and experiences. They showed a clear sense of career purpose and pride.

It's tough out there

How can you be sure that your resume will make the cut? Probably never before in your lifetime has that question been so critical to job candidates. In just a few years, this country has gone from having a surplus of jobs to having a growing surplus of candidates. People are afraid to leave college because those recruiters aren't comin' a courtin' college grads the way they were just a few short years ago. Those already in jobs are afraid to leave them. They do not have as much confidence that they will find anything else.

Does that mean that *nobody* is getting hired? Of course not. But it does mean that for candidates even to get in to see employers, their resumes must deliver on both form and function, or, to put it another way, good looks and content.

What this book will teach you

As the old saying goes, nothing succeeds like success. The resumes in this book are all winners. They landed candidates jobs and they were remembered—sometimes many years later—by some of the most successful and well-known recruiters, outplacement firms, personnel agencies and career experts in the country.

Standing out in such a way surely will get your resume over the 20-second hurdle.

However, we don't want you simply to *copy* the resumes you'll find here. So, the first part of this book will provide you good, solid advice on how to think about your qualifications, skills, experience and education and put together a winning resume.

Chapter 1 will talk a little bit about how you should think about your resume—as an advertisement or direct-mail piece with which you are hoping to sell *you*.

Chapter 2 will talk about the various approaches you can take in writing a resume and just how to determine exactly which is the best approach for you, whether you are just getting out of school or a veteran of the work force. While this chapter strongly stresses that no two resumes should look alike, it provides some firm guidelines on items that you should *never* include.

Chapter 3 will discuss the various resume formats from which you can choose—chronological, functional or a combination. Chapter 4 will talk about the contents—what the employer really wants to know.

Chapter 5 will provide more do's and don'ts so that your resume will be easy to read, polished and professional.

Chapter 6 echoes the famous advice that Ernest Hemingway had for authors: Write standing up. Edit sitting down. This chapter talks about how to make yourself sound more intelligent than even *you* thought you were.

And then comes the section that puts this book in a class by itself, real-life resumes that are the talk of the recruiting establishment. We asked job hunting and career professionals for the best resumes they'd ever seen and the reasons why they stood out.

The largest section of this book delivers those resumes and explanations. Taking the advice we provide in the first section of this book and then comparing your efforts to the resumes you'll find here will help you put together a resume that will be remembered by employers with just the right job for you.

Good luck!

Chapter 9 echoes the famous advice that Ernest Hemingway had for writers: Write standing up. Edit sitting down. This chapter talks about how to make yourself sound more intelligent than even you thought you were.

And then comes the section that puts this book in a class by itself: real-life resumes that are the talk of the recruiting establishment. We asked job hunting and career professionals for the best resumes they'd ever seen, and the reasons why they stood out.

The largest section of this book delivers those resumes and explanations. Taking the advice we provide in the first section of this book and then comparing your efforts to the resumes you'll find here will help you put together a resume that will be remembered by employers with just the right job for you.

Good luck!

Chapter 1

The Product? You. The Advertisement? Your Resume!

Think for a minute about the best magazine advertisement you ever saw.

Why did the marketer spend the money and the time to place that ad in front of you? What did it accomplish? Why?

First, the ad made you stop and read what the marketer had to say. When you opened that copy of *Newsweek*, *Rolling Stone*, *Vogue* or *Sports Illustrated*, perhaps the last thing you wanted to do was shop. But, thanks to a picture, a headline, a color, a layout, you stopped reading long enough to give that marketer some of your time, probably the most precious commodity in the late 20th century.

Time is on my side

That's precisely what you want your resume to do—buy a little time from prospective employers, pique their interest so that they will give your resume a little more attention than they do other candidates and perhaps commit to devoting even more time to getting to know you better.

In this light, then, your resume is an advertisement for *you*. It must describe you and it must suit you.

By the latter, we mean that *form* must fit *content*. You wouldn't expect an ad for Diet Pepsi to look like one for Preparation H (or vice versa). Yet, some creative directors might very well have resumes that look like bankers' resumes and some bankers might come up with resumes that look like those of art dealers. In such cases, the form of the resume would be setting up a false expectation with the customer (the employer) and defeat the purpose of putting together the resume in the first place.

A resume must scream out, "This is who I am. This is what I want to do in my career." It must intrigue the potential employer. And it must convince him or her that *you* are worth further investigation.

So, now you're ready to write?

Okay, so just describe yourself and what you want to do and there you'll have it—the perfect resume.

Except it's not that easy.

Getting back to our advertisement analogy, you first must develop a really good feel for the product, must sincerely believe in it and know it, or the ad will ring false.

Just how do you get to know yourself a little better so that you can market yourself effectively? Take stock.

You'll have to gather or remember information about your:

- Work or internship experience.
- Education (high school, college and graduate school).
- Special training (seminars, certifications, licensing, etc.).
- Military experience.
- Volunteer experience.
- Skills.
- Awards and honors.
- Memberships and activities (both professional and social).

In order to organize this material, set up the worksheets described next and shown at the end of this chapter.

Work experience: Go on, sell 'em

Write down the most salient details of every job you've held. And that means *every* job—selling hot dogs at the ballpark as well as some high-level executive position that landed you an office with a window. If you've been working for several years or more, pay particular attention to your most recent positions, but don't dismiss part-time jobs or those you held early on in your career.

First, put down the nitty-gritty details of these positions, including:

- Each employer's name, address and telephone number.
- Names of supervisors.
- Exact dates worked at each company.
- Approximate number of hours per week.
- Specific duties and responsibilities (what you did on the job).
- Specific skills utilized.
- Awards, letters of recommendation.

Okay, now take another look at what you *did* at those jobs. What's probably coming to mind are phrases like, "edited copy" or "made sales calls" or "designed widgets." But will phrases like these add up to exciting advertising copy? Do Diet Pepsi's ads merely state that it is a soft drink?

In putting together your resume, it's more important to think about what you *accomplished*. Your job descriptions on this worksheet should contain phrases like these:

- Developed new standards for editing, which led to magazine's winning an award.
- Improved a computer-aided design system for refining widget plans.
- Achieved record year in Sheboygan, Wis., territory.

Do these sound pretty good to you? Well, they should be better. You should give these accomplishments more thought. Whenever possible, state the benefits in precise, objective terms—numbers are good for providing that element of precision.

- Refined computer-aided design system that improved productivity of department 31%.

If you list a work-related award or honor, think about what's special about it. Were you one of only three people to receive it? How would you make it sound important to someone unfamiliar with your field?

Many of you are probably thinking, "But I've never accomplished *anything* on the job."

We don't buy that. Look at some of the evaluations you've received from your superiors (yes, you should have held on to those). Or think about promotions you've gotten and why you deserved them.

You also should think back to some of the big projects your department handled. What role did you play in those projects? And what about the day-to-day job you did? How did the company benefit from having you on the payroll?

Volunteer experience

Some candidates seem to have the mentality of an appraiser: "If something is free, it has no value." But the fact is your unpaid volunteer experience can be a gold mine for great resume marketing copy.

Whatever your volunteer experience, you can turn it into valuable "sales copy" on your resume. This is particularly valuable for people with little or no work experience or for those people, such as homemakers, who are returning to the work force after a somewhat lengthy hiatus. Were you captain of the football team or president of the 4-H club? Have you been a coach of the local Little League team or involved in your church's charitable activities?

This translates into valuable work-related experience—even if you didn't get paid for it.

The old saying, "If you want something done, give it to a busy person," connotes that employers love people who are "doers." Your *active* participation in volunteer organizations will show that you are such a busy person.

Therefore, you should note your volunteer experience on a worksheet the same way you would your paid work experience.

First, include the following:

- Each organization's name, address and telephone number.
- Name of the paid director or the voluntary leader you worked with.
- Exact dates when you were involved in the organization.
- Approximate number of hours you spent doing things for the organization per week.
- Specific duties and responsibilities.
- Specific skills used.
- Awards, letters of recommendation.

Describe your responsibilities and accomplishments in professional terms. Again, think of how you can *quantify* the experience so that your membership appears to be more than something you did in name only. Did you manage a fund drive? Create a new program? Increase membership 20 percent? Handle the budget?

If you've been a long-time member of an organization, describe your climb through the ranks the same way you would your job history.

Again, you want to talk in terms of *accomplishments*, rather than just deeds. This worksheet should have phrases that read like these:

- Helped organize the first girls' soccer team in Glen Ridge. Recruited coaches, arranged for sponsorships for six teams, gained the participation of 72 girls.
- Helped raise $50,000 for United Way's annual drive in Altoona. Recruited telephone marketing volunteers, wrote scripts, helped coordinate direct-mail effort.

Even if you never had the time to become a leader at your organization, think of the ways in which you contributed and how important your actions were to the accomplishments of the entire organization. Did you help organize the annual picnic? Create items for sale at the crafts fair? Drive the bus for the high-school band? Don't overlook these activities that portray you as a *doer*.

Education

For those who have been working for some time, the details of academic life are relatively unimportant. However, for those on the job less than five years, education history is a critical component of the resume.

We've seen many resumes from recent graduates that were filled with what amounted to long lists of the courses they'd taken in school. But, just as a listing of job responsibilities will put a potential employer to sleep, so, too, will a listing of courses. You must add a little sizzle to the steak by telling the employer what exactly you accomplished in school.

First things first, write down these details about the high school, college and graduate school you attended:

- Name, address and telephone number of each school.
- Years attended.

- Degrees earned.
- Major field of study.
- Minor field of study.
- Honors.
- Important courses.

What kind of accomplishments can you talk about in this worksheet? Well, if you maintained a 3.8 grade point average while earning 50 percent of your college expenses, that would certainly convince an employer that you are a can-do person. Or, you might have won a fellowship to graduate school, been named a research assistant to a leading authority in your field of study, participated in a large number of extracurricular activities, been elected to a high post in student government.

If you did participate in many extracurriculars, then set up a special worksheet for these. Provide the following details:

- Name, address and telephone number of the organization.
- Office(s) you held.
- Duties/responsibilities with the organization.
- Number of hours you were involved in the organization per week.

Other training, military service, special skills

Did you attend courses with the American Management Association? Have you had on-the-job training from your employer in computer technology or other specialty? Then set up a special worksheet to detail such specialized training.

If you've had a stint with Uncle Sam in the military, set up a worksheet with details concerning your tour of duty and, again, your accomplishments.

Do you have any special skills that the other worksheets have not provided room to expound upon? Perhaps you speak a foreign language fluently or have a particular affinity for working with computers. Then, set up a worksheet headed, "Special Skills," on which you can detail:

- Name of the skill.
- Specific training received in that specialty.
- Years of experience you've had working in the area.
- Your level of expertise.
- Accomplishments related to this skill.

To sum it all up

After you've completed all of these worksheets, summarize your various skills on yet another piece of paper. Write down the total number of years' experience you have performing particular tasks (perhaps you've been a sales executive for eight years, or, with your volunteer experience, have 14 years of experience handling a budget).

These skills should fit into areas that correspond to "real jobs in the real world" such as accounting, computer operations, management, public relations, editing, sales and marketing, and teaching.

In the introduction of this book, we talked about a review of resumes that we did at our company. While we were going through the stack of hopefuls, we were not merely looking for sparkling documents, but for descriptions of candidates who would fulfill a *need* that our company had. Therefore, the best resume will tell the employer that you've got what he or she wants, that you can solve a problem. The following chapters will discuss how to engineer a resume that will do just that.

1. Work Experience

(Make one copy of this worksheet for each paid job or professional internship position you have held.)

1. Name of company__________

2. Address and phone number__________

3. Your job title (Use the actual title that would be on employee records.)__________

4. Start and end dates (month and year)__________

5. Salary (beginning and end)__________

6. Supervisor's name and title__________

7. General job description (one- or two-sentence summary of your job)__________

8. Responsibilities

   Management/supervisory duties (include size of staff and specific duties—hiring, training, etc.)__________

   Budgetary/financial duties (include any duties related to money—writing a budget, totaling daily receipts, analyzing cost/profit ratios, etc.)__________

   Sales/marketing duties (include specifics about product sold, type of customer base, advertising responsibilities, long-term marketing planning, etc.)__________

Customer service (include number of customers you served on a regular basis, plus their "status"—retail customer, executive-level clients, etc.)

Production duties (include amount of goods/services produced on a daily, monthly or annual basis)

Technical duties (include any duties that required you to use computers or other technical equipment)

Other

9. Accomplishments (include honors and awards)

10. Special skills learned (computer skills, telephone sales, desktop publishing, etc.)

2. Volunteer Experience

(Make one copy of this worksheet for each volunteer position you have held.)

1. Name of organization__________

2. Address and phone number__________

3. Position/title (if no position held, simply indicate "member")__________

4. Start and end dates of this position__________

5. Start and end dates of your membership (month and year)__________

6. Hours devoted per week__________

7. Name(s) of organization president(s) or your ranking superior__________

8. General description (one or two sentence summary of your job)__________

9. Responsibilities

   Management/supervisory duties (include size of staff and specific duties—coordinating, training, etc.)__________

   Budgetary/financial duties (include any duties related to money—writing a budget, totaling sales receipts, analyzing cost/profit ratios, etc.)__________

   Sales/marketing duties (include specifics about product sold, type of customer base, advertising responsibilities, long-term marketing planning, etc.)__________

Customer service (include number of "customers" you contacted on a regular basis, plus their "status"—high school students, disabled adults, community leaders, etc.)

Production duties (include amount of goods/services produced on a daily, monthly or annual basis)

Technical duties (any duties that required you to use computers or other technical equipment)

Other

10. Accomplishments (include honors and awards)

11. Special skills learned (computer skills, telephone sales, desktop publishing, etc.)

3. Education

High school education

(If you have many years of experience under your belt, you need only complete questions 1-6 for high school education.)

1. School name__________
2. Address (city and state)__________
3. Years attended__________
4. Year graduated__________
5. GPA/class rank__________
6. Honors (valedictorian, Top 10%, scholarship recipient, etc.)__________
7. Accomplishments__________
8. Major courses__________
9. Special skills learned__________

Post-secondary education

(List here college, trade school and postgraduate work.)

1. School name__________
2. Address (city and state)__________
3. Years attended__________
4. Year graduated and degree earned__________
5. GPA/class rank__________
6. Honors (valedictorian, scholarship recipient, etc.)__________
7. Accomplishments__________
8. Major courses__________
9. Special skills learned__________

4. Other Training

(List here any additional vocational courses, on-job training, licenses or certification.)

1. Training received/license or certification earned__________

2. Name of training institution__________
3. Address and phone number__________

4. Start and end dates of training__________
5. Name and title of instructor__________
6. Skills learned__________

7. Accomplishments__________

---

1. Training received/license or certification earned__________

2. Name of training institution__________
3. Address and phone number__________

4. Start and end dates of training__________
5. Name and title of instructor__________
6. Skills learned__________

7. Accomplishments__________

---

1. Training received/license or certification earned__________

2. Name of training institution__________
3. Address and phone number__________

4. Start and end dates of training__________
5. Name and title of instructor__________
6. Skills learned__________

7. Accomplishments__________

5. Military Service

1. Branch________________
2. Rank________________
3. Dates of service________________
4. Duties________________
5. Special skills learned________________
6. Accomplishments (include awards, citations, medals)________________

6. Special Skills

1. Name of skill________________
2. Specific training received________________
3. Years of experience________________
4. Level of expertise________________
5. Accomplishments related to this skill________________

1. Name of skill________________
2. Specific training received________________
3. Years of experience________________
4. Level of expertise________________
5. Accomplishments related to this skill________________

1. Name of skill________________
2. Specific training received________________
3. Years of experience________________
4. Level of expertise________________
5. Accomplishments related to this skill________________

7. Skills Summary

Skill Area______________________________

Years Experience in this Area____________________

Special Training______________________________

Accomplishments______________________________

Skill Area______________________________

Years Experience in this Area____________________

Special Training______________________________

Accomplishments______________________________

Skill Area______________________________

Years Experience in this Area____________________

Special Training______________________________

Accomplishments______________________________

Skill Area______________________________

Years Experience in this Area____________________

Special Training______________________________

Accomplishments______________________________

Chapter 2

Resume Form and Substance

Right about now, you're probably itching to sit at the word processor and start your resume. But before you do that, you should first consider the many options you have to fashion your resume so that it reflects the real you.

And, indeed, there are a wealth of options, both in format and in types of sections you can include or omit. Again, thinking of your resume as an advertisement, you should consider how the form of your resume fits what you're selling.

For instance, a product that's been on the market a long time ideally would have an ad that talks about longevity as an indication of quality and appeal. Think about the ads for Keds sneakers that position them simply as "what to wear."

However, a new kid on the block needs a totally different type of ad package. Its strengths are unknown and unproven. Ads for such products must make a splash, but talk about the care that went into their development. Think about the ads for the Saturn cars from GM.

As we found in putting together this book, there certainly is no one right way to create a resume. Ask—as we did—dozens of experts to pick the perfect resume and you'll come up with more variety than you'd find on the menu of a good all-night diner.

Some prospective employees have a lot of experience to brag about; others have none. Some have worked for some of the leading companies in their field, while other candidates have accomplished a great deal, but at relatively obscure operations. Some candidates have B.A.s from Brown, M.B.A.s from Harvard and Ph.D.s from Wharton, while others worked to pay their expenses while attending St. Mary of the Plains.

All of these candidates will—or *should*—have quite different types of resumes. Because, after all, there is only one resume format that's *right*. It's the one that best displays your skills and qualifications and shows the employer that there's a good fit between your qualities and his or her needs.

Don't write a resume without...

Okay, so before we discuss the various option packages available, let's talk about the resume elements that you absolutely cannot drive away without.

1. **Name, address and telephone number.** Yes, believe it or not, we have received resumes lacking one or two of these three essentials. And we've gotten resumes on which the telephone number was wrong or the address was a post office box. So, to make doubly sure that you don't forget these elements, put them right at the top of your resume.
2. **Skills and experience.** This is the flesh and blood of the resume, the reason you'll be looked at carefully or passed by. Even if you are just getting out of school and about to embark on your first job hunt, include something here so that the employer will see that you've got what he or she *needs*.
3. **Education and training.** The length of this section will be in inverse proportion to the amount of on-the-job experience you have. But even if you're Bill Clinton, you'll want to have some mention of your education on your resume. (Can we ever forget that he went to Oxford and inhaled all that culture?)

Resume options

That's it for the "must have's"—the four wheels, brakes, engine and driver's seat of your resume. But is this the resume you want to be seen around town in?

Perhaps not just yet. You have several options to choose from that can be very useful in some situations.

1. Job objective

Some career counselors and human resources executives would tell you that the job objective—a brief statement that tells the employer the type of job you want—is essential. Others will tell you it's a restatement of the obvious and a waste of valuable space.

Before we examine the pros and cons, let's first examine what a job objective paragraph typically should look like.

> **Objective:** A position in a sales organization with a well-structured training program in which I can use and develop communications and administrative skills.

Those in the pro-objective camp will tell you that such sections tell employers exactly what you want and that you have a good handle on your career goals. In addition, it tells the busy recruiter or hiring manager, at a glance, exactly what position you're after (the recipient of your resume might have 10 job searches going on simultaneously).

However, this strength of the job objective is also its very weakness. Let's say you have been researching companies at which you'd love to work and saw that a position had opened at XYZ Computer Solutions. While the fact is that, with a degree in computer science, you'd like to land *any* entry-level position at XYZ, you include on your resume a job objective that positions you for the technical sales representative opening you heard about.

The problem with the job objective in such a case is that, even though you know you're interested in other jobs at XYZ, the screener in the HR department won't.

Remember, also, that a resume is supposed to depict you as the person who can fill an employer's needs. But a job-objective paragraph right up front is talking about what *you* want. It would be as if Michelin said, "We hope you'll buy our tires so that we can get rich and retire at 48," rather than, "Buy Michelin to protect what you love the most."

However, there are two very specific types of situations in which it would be absolutely foolish *not* to include a job objective:

1. **When there is one job out there with your name on it.** You are absolutely bound and determined to be an editor on a newspaper's sports desk. Then go for it. State the precise objective you have and be as specific as possible. Will only a big-city sports desk do? Some will be impressed by your focus on a career goal. But you might be closing some doors that, eventually, would lead you to your ideal job.
2. **When it would be difficult for a potential employer to decipher your career goal** unless you spell it out. Let's suppose you're in transition, that you want to take the skills you've learned on one job and parlay them into a brand-new career. For instance, let's say you have vast experience in direct marketing, but would now like to become involved in fund raising for a nonprofit organization. Because your work history might not reflect that new interest, establish it up front. For instance, in such a situation the objective might read:

   > To use knowledge and experience in direct mail and telemarketing techniques and list selection to solicit donations for a nonprofit, charitable enterprise.

2. Summary of qualifications

Like a job objective, a summary of a candidate's skills appears at the very beginning of the resume, before any information is given about experience or education.

Just as the job objective option can tell an employer where you want to go, the summary of qualifications can give a very solid indication of where you've been and what you've done. It is a snapshot, a two-or three-phrase career in a nutshell. Here are a couple of examples:

> **Summary:** Completing degree in journalism, with a minor in marketing. Interned as assistant account executive with copywriting responsibilities at local advertising agency. Sold advertising space for college newspaper.

> **Summary:** Sixteen years of editing and writing experience as well as three years of experience managing advertising sales, promotion, production and circulation. Winner of the Jesse H. Neal Award for Journalistic Excellence.

These summaries can sound pretty good, but should you include one in your resume?

Again, the field of experts is divided. Some say that such paragraphs are straight from the Department of Redundancy Department, that an employer should be able to formulate his or her own summary from reading about your experience and education.

That's certainly true. However, given the fact that you have to catch the busy screener's attention within 20 seconds, the summary may be a smart way to advertise.

The well-written summary has the same impact as the headline on an effective print advertisement. It will catch the screener's attention and convince him or her to read on. In a small amount of space, the summary can:

1. Let you showcase areas of expertise that match the employer's needs. If, for instance, a classified ad indicates that management experience is essential for the successful candidate, put a summary at the top of your resume, which encapsulates all of the supervisory know-how you've developed.

2. Unearth some of the pearls that might be overlooked in the body of your resume. This is particularly the case if it is a two-page resume detailing several previous jobs.

3. Make the whole of your experience more impressive than the sum of the parts. If you are trying to showcase your management expertise that you've gained in several jobs, do the adding up of your experience for the employer. State that you have "seven years of advertising sales experience" rather than hoping that the employer arrives at this impressive statistic himself.

Remember that the summary is helpful only when you actually have something to sum up. If you're just entering the job market or have held your current job for less than a year, a qualifications summary will look absolutely ludicrous.

3. Volunteer experience

Some career experts would argue that including volunteer experience on your resume is strictly optional, but we would strongly disagree, *especially* if you don't have much on-the-job experience. As discussed in the last chapter, volunteer activities that enabled you to *accomplish* something, that allow you to demonstrate an important skill to a prospective employer, are key components of a complete resume.

4. Outside interests

Perhaps it's unfair for us to write about this option since we have such a visceral dislike for sentences such as "I like jazz, reading and going to museums" on resumes.

Of course, there are exceptions. If you're going for a job as a fitness trainer, your interest in aerobics and running will be of interest to a prospective employer. If you're applying for a job with a catering firm, your love of cooking will be a plus. And, if you are trying to get a job as a road manager for the Grateful Dead, it might help if your resume talked about the two years you followed the band around the world.

But for the most part, let your personality and your real life come through during *interviews*. Why risk *not* getting an interview because your resume gives a prospective employer the notion that you spend your free time frivolously?

5. Awards and honors

Include only those awards that you received as a result of your work, your volunteer activities or your academic performance, and only those relevant to the job you're seeking.

Mentioning appropriate awards will be the equivalent of a management "Good Housekeeping Seal of Approval." If a manager thinks well of you, you'll have an edge if he or she sees that other managers did, too.

6. Professional and social affiliations

If you've been in the job market awhile and are committed to your career, you may have joined at least one trade association or professional society.

Therefore, you risk looking uninterested in your career if you don't list memberships in these organizations. However, you shouldn't include organizations for which involvement for you has meant little or nothing more than paying your annual dues. If you're asked about these affiliations during an interview, you'll have to admit that you really haven't been involved in the association at all.

Be even more circumspect about including social clubs and organizations on your resume. If you are applying for a job to a manager who is a dyed-in-the-wool Democrat, do you want your affiliation with the Young Republicans to close the door on any hope for working for him?

On the other hand, if you are trying to market the experience you've gained in working with these organizations, you may want to include them. Even in such cases, choose carefully. Avoid mentioning controversial causes unless you want to work only for people who will sympathize with your beliefs and you want to test them early.

Are these options? No way!

We began this chapter, you'll remember, with a list of the elements that you absolutely *must* include on your resume. Now, we are going to tell you about seven deadly resume sins—things you should *never* include.

1. **The word "resume."** Let's face it, you probably wouldn't want to work for anyone who didn't recognize a resume as a resume. Don't waste the space. Use it to tell the prospective employer one more scintillating detail about yourself.

2. **Salary information.** Sometimes employers specifically request "salary history" or "salary requirements" of applicants. But you should never include your income history on your resume. It can either eliminate you from consideration (if you make "too much") before you ever get in the

door, or it can tell the employer that he or she can get you cheap. These are not the types of signals you want your resume to send.

3. **Job references.** Again, this is information that can be included on a separate sheet. Some people write, "References available upon request" toward the end of their resumes, but this is unnecessary. Few employers are about to hire a candidate who can't produce a good reference or two.

4. **Testimonials.** Yes, we've seen resumes that contain quotes like, "Produced an advertisement that David Ogilvy said was the best he'd ever seen." Or, "Managing editor said that she would have worked with me forever if it hadn't been for that huge layoff." This will do absolutely no good. After all, how much credence can such comments have when every employer knows you wouldn't include negative comments on your resume? Or would you?

   If, however, a former employer did say that you were the greatest thing since work was invented, bring copies of testimonial letters along with you to the interview.

5. **Personal statistics.** In this day and age of lawsuits, it is not advisable to put information about your looks, marital status, familial status or health on your resume. Such information as, "Married, with two children. 5'11", 185 lbs. In excellent health," should not stand you in better stead with an employer, unless the employer wants to face a discrimination suit.

   It's better to fill this valuable space with information about your *job* qualifications rather than with facts about your personal life that should be irrelevant to today's employer.

6. **Personality profiles.** We can't wait until we get a resume that describes a candidate something like this: "Have difficulty facing anyone before third cup of coffee. Although fun most of the time, can be moody."

   It would be ridiculous to own up to such character flaws on a resume, wouldn't it? Of course. Therefore, phrases like, "excellent self-starter," "highly motivated" and, an all-time favorite, "enthusiastic," don't carry much weight.

7. **Photographs.** Are you trying to get onto the cover of *Vogue*? If so, then you should probably send a photo along with your resume. After all, your looks are an important qualification for the type of work you're looking for.

   If not, you're asking employers to do something that is patently illegal—making a hiring decision on the basis of looks. Don't put a prospective employer in that position—and yourself at a disadvantage—by doing something so unprofessional.

Now that we've discussed all of the do's and don'ts, it's time to discuss how you should organize all of the options you choose into an attention-getting, job-landing resume.

Chapter 3

Format Options: Which Works Best for *You*?

Before you begin feverishly writing your resume, hold on. You still have some more options to choose from, all of them having to do with format.

There are essentially three types of formats from which to choose:

1. **The chronological resume** organizes your employment and educational history by date (most recent first). This is usually the obvious choice for those who've been in the job market for some time, and it is the format for the vast majority of all resumes.
2. **The functional resume** is an expanded summary of qualifications. It devotes a great deal of space to the duties and responsibilities of all the jobs an applicant has held over the course of a career.
3. **The combination resume** is a bit of both. Some candidates with very specific jobs in mind will begin their resumes with a functional-style listing of relevant skills and accomplishments before launching into their employment histories.

The chronological resume

There's some good news and some bad news for those electing this format. The good news: It is the "safe" choice. Most candidates use it and employers feel comfortable with this type of presentation of employment and academic information.

The bad news: It will be tough to have your resume stand out from the crowd.

Using a chronological format, you would detail the various positions you've held during your career, beginning with the most recent and working backward. For each position, provide the following information:

- Employer's name and location.
- Dates of your employment (month and year of start and end dates are sufficient).
- Position(s) held at each company.
- Responsibilities and accomplishments in those positions.

In most cases, this information comprises about 70 percent of the resume and is delivered right after the job objective and skills summary sections, if included.

However, some candidates choose to place their educational credentials first, deeming these their most important qualification for the job they are seeking.

Of course, this format is also useful for detailing volunteer experience. You would simply list volunteer positions in the same manner as you would paid positions, providing the organization's name, the years of your involvement with the organization, your position and your responsibilities and accomplishments.

The chronological resume works best when all or most of the following apply:

1. You have a history of employment or volunteer work that shows stability.
2. You've been working in the same field for awhile and are seeking another position in that area.
3. You have had a steady upward progression of titles and levels of responsibility throughout your working life.
4. You have not been a job-hopper and have been able to endure at least one year with every employer you've had.

The functional resume

For many people, the chronological resume spells disaster. It can shed unflattering light on a history of job-hopping and reveal a career progression that resembled a zigzagging road through hill country, rather than a ladder straight to the top.

The functional resume, on the other hand, can smooth out these rough spots.

Essentially the functional resume format allows you to group accomplishments, qualifications and experience—your key selling points—together. The format can help you play up your experience in specialty areas.

As some of the career experts cited later in this book will tell you, functional resumes are not welcomed with open arms in the employment world. Some employers view them as "problem resumes" because they believe the candidate has chosen the format to hide some glaring flaws or deficiencies.

Some career experts and employers also object instinctively because the names and dates of employment are played down as if, here again, the candidate were trying to hide something.

Nevertheless, despite the objections, you owe it to yourself to consider the functional resume if:

1. Your work history does not exactly match your new career goals.
2. You don't have a great deal of experience related specifically to the position you seek. Hence, you want to play up some of your other strengths.
3. You have noticeable gaps in your employment history.

The combination resume

To overcome employer objections to the functional resume yet allow you to position yourself in as positive a light as possible, you may want to use a combination format—taking the best parts of both functional and chronological formats. For example, if you have little professional sales experience and you're seeking a job as a salesperson, you might want to lead off with a functional-style listing of customer-service credentials and community service accomplishments—items that will demonstrate good, face-to-face "people skills." Then, you could launch into the chronological listing of employment, volunteer work and education.

The choice is yours

Perhaps the best thing to do in order to determine the right format for your resume is to put yourself in the employer's shoes. Consider:

1. If you were the employer, what would you want *most* from the person you're hiring? What would be the first thing you'd look for on the resume? The right degree? The right job experience? A long history in the industry?
2. What will the employer see as your very best qualifications for the job? Will it be education? Special training you've received? Proof of management expertise?

The answers to these questions will help you formulate a resume that will produce results.

Chapter 4

Time to Write Your First Draft

At last! It's time to take all of the lessons learned in the first three chapters of this book and begin *writing* your resume. The most fundamental rule of resume writing is that you must lead with your best foot, emphasizing the skills, experience and technical knowledge that will most help you get the job you want. Remember the prospective employer out there has a need, and you're out to convince him or her that you can fill it.

In resume-writing it is essential that you make every word count. The screeners, recruiters and hiring managers you're trying to appeal to won't have the patience for long-windedness or verbal meandering. Say what you have to say clearly and concisely.

And, at least as you're putting together your first draft, don't feel that you have to be perfect. Be more concerned with communicating to prospective employers, rather than having a perfect style. You'll have a chance to polish it later.

The ideal resume length?

Myth: A resume should *never* be more than one page long.

Fact: Your resume must be as succinct as possible, but long enough to adequately relay your experience and qualifications. Thus, if you've just entered the work force and your job experience is scarce, one page will probably be plenty of room for you to spell out your skills.

If you've been in the work force for several years and have accumulated a variety of valuable experiences, then by all means take two pages to communicate this to prospective employers. Don't sell yourself short by cutting out impressive qualifications to squeeze your resume onto one page.

But, as a rule, we don't recommend going over two pages. Most employers simply won't read anything longer, unless they're searching for a high-level executive. What's more, most employers think that candidates who cannot limit themselves to a two-page resume lack essential organizational and communication skills.

Yet, rules are meant to be broken. And, as you'll see in the second half of this book, the experts will give you a wide range of answers. For recruitment guru Robert Half, the ideal resume is short and sweet. In fact, the best resume he ever saw (you'll see it on page 98) is only *36 words* long!

However, Barbara Provus, principal and cofounder of Shepherd Bueschel & Provus, Inc., likes best the resume weighing in at *four pages* that you'll see on pages 148 to 151.

Watch your language

One way to assure that your resume is not overly "windy" is to write it in a telegraph style. Don't use full sentences. Instead, begin each entry with an arresting action word. Of course, you should avoid using words over and over or you'll seem to be terribly uncreative. Dust off your thesaurus and look for a wide variety of words to describe your responsibilities.

To help you out a bit with choosing the best resume-*ese*, here is a list of some of the action words you can choose from to give power to your resume:

accomplished
achieved
adjusted
administered
advised
analyzed
approved
arranged
assisted
budgeted
built
calculated
charted
compared
compiled
completed
composed
conducted
consolidated
constructed
consulted
controlled
conceptualized
coordinated
counseled
created
decreased
delivered
designated
designed
detected
determined
developed
devised
diagnosed
directed
discovered
distributed
edited
eliminated
enlarged
established
evaluated
examined
expanded
formulated
founded
flagged
gathered
generated
guided
headed
identified
implemented
improved
increased
initiated
inspected
installed
instituted
instructed
interpreted
invented
justified
lectured
led
lobbied
maintained
managed
modified
motivated
negotiated
obtained
operated
organized
ordered
overhauled
performed
persuaded
planned
prepared
presented
presided
processed
produced
programmed
promoted
proposed
provided
purchased
recommended
reduced
referred
regulated
reorganized
replaced
reported
represented
researched
restored
reviewed
revised
scheduled
selected
served
sold
solved
studied
supervised
supplied
systematized
taught
tested
traced
trained
translated
updated
utilized
won
wrote

The Chronological Resume

1. The header

The header, which tells employers your name and how they can reach you, should always be the first thing on the first page of your resume. Set the header—or at least your name—in boldface type at the center of the page so that it is very prominent.

Include your full name (or at least first and last name with middle initials) and, even if you've been called Rusty or some other sobriquet your entire life, don't use a nickname. Of course, it's essential to include your address and phone number. If you are employed, include your daytime and evening phone numbers. However, if you are unable to accept confidential phone calls at your job, include only your home phone number, but make sure to attach an answering machine. It's unlikely that employers will call you after office hours.

If you are at a temporary address, indicate where you can be reached after a certain date.

2. The job objective (optional)

If you decide to include a job objective, include it right under the header. Set the objective off with the headline, "Objective," "Job Objective" or "Career Objective."

When writing your objective, avoid the trap that so many job seekers fall into—using vague words and phrases that really don't add up to much. If you are going to write an objective like the one below, don't bother to include one.

> To obtain a position in a progressive company where I can use my skills to increase sales and contribute to the overall success of the organization.

Instead, spell out exactly what you are looking for. Be strong, confident, focused and concise.

> To direct a sales organization at a consumer products company.

> To obtain a position in an architectural firm specializing in industrial interiors.

That tells the employer *what* you want to do. The rest of the resume tells the employer *how* you will do it if you're hired.

3. The skills summary (optional)

If you decide to include this element on your resume, place it directly under the header or the job objective. Set it off with a headline such as "Skills Summary," "Experience Summary" or "Summary of Qualifications." You can present this summary in a single paragraph or in a series of bulleted points.

Why are you including the summary? It is a good way to catch an employer's attention and make him or her want to read more about you. But don't overdo it! If you decide on a paragraph style, use two or three short sentences. For instance:

Summary of Qualifications: Supervised account teams working on major consumer products advertising campaigns. Seven years of copywriting and creative supervisory experience. Master's in marketing.

If you choose to use bullets, include no more than four or five items. For example:

- 16 years in association management.
- Expertise in convention management, publishing and membership development.
- Winner of Innovator award from U.S. Society of Association Executives.
- Strong background in advertising, telecommunications associations.

Include your most salient strength first. If you have, say, two key strengths, each of which might be more important to different types of employers, do two resumes.

4. Experience

Experience, goes the old saying, is the best teacher. Hence it's this section of your resume that employers are most interested in and to which you should devote the most space.

The first thing to consider is whether you want to group paid and volunteer positions or list them separately. It's probably a good idea to group them if you don't have a great deal of paid experience under your belt just yet.

If you do that, a good heading for the section might be, "Professional and Volunteer Experience," or simply "Experience."

The only problem is, if you've held volunteer and paid positions simultaneously, putting them into a chronological format might confuse an employer.

Most people include only paid positions in the Experience section, then follow with their volunteer activities and memberships.

The listing of your positions should look something like this:

Gordion Wire Co., Waukesha, Wis.
Director of Research, 1988-present.
Developed strategy for company's entry into international markets. Supervised staff of two research assistants. Examined implications of foreign exchange fluctuations, various political situations and availabilities of adequate distribution channels. Findings led to company's entry into Pacific Rim.

Employees who've held several jobs with one company, thanks to promotions, have something great to brag about on their resumes. Yet, most such candidates do a very poor job of enhancing this positive selling point on their resumes.

Here's the best way to present such a history:

Crown Distribution Company, La Jolla, Calif., July 1985-present.
Director of Sales and Marketing, 1990 to present. Oversee sales activities of 60 representatives throughout U.S. and Canada. Direct-marketing and publicity strategies.

- Increased national sales 15% annually.
- Developed Clio Award-winning television advertising campaign.

Eastern District Sales Director, June 1987-June 1990. Supervised sales activities in 22 Eastern states. Personally handled all company's Eastern-based national accounts, comprising 48 percent of company's total revenues.

- Increased sales in territory 92 percent in four years and more than doubled market share.

Sales Executive, July 1985-June 1987. In charge of sales in Middle Atlantic. Increased sales in territory 42 percent in two years.

- Won company's Salesman of the Year Award in 1985 and 1986.

As you can see in this example, the chronological format requires that you list your most recent position first. The more recently you've held a position, the more information you should provide.

Best for first

What you say about each of the individual listings on your resume depends on the importance and recency of the position. For the most recent positions, provide:

- Name of employer.
- Employer's location.
- Your dates of employment.
- Your position or job title.
- A summary of your responsibilities.
- Your major accomplishments.

Be sure to provide *all* of this information for the first four to six positions appearing on the resume, or for the first seven to 10 years of on-the-job experience. Once you've done that, describe in full only those positions that strengthen your sales pitch. If you were the youngest person to be promoted to a position, or if you achieved a particularly noteworthy accomplishment, then it's worth describing some job out of the misty past. Otherwise, provide only the employer's name and location, your position and the dates of employment.

A matter of style

Here's the best way to present these various components of your experience listings:

Employer or organization name and location. Always state the full name of the company, rather than using acronyms that might not be familiar to your prospective new employer. General Motors, for instance, should not be called "GM." However, 3M—well known by that name—should not be called Minnesota Mining and Minerals.

Dates of employment. Indicate the month and year you began and left each position. If you've been in the work force a long time and kept each of your jobs a year or more, you can consider leaving off the months.

Job title. Avoid the temptation to give yourself a promotion so that you look better to a prospective employer. However, by all means, use commonly used job titles if a company you've worked for has used particularly idiosyncratic ones. For instance, if your company uses a title like "group leader," you might substitute the more-commonly used "supervisor."

Description of responsibilities. Keep it brief. Sum up your major responsibilities in broad terms. Remember, you don't need to explain to a company seeking a customer service representative what a customer service representative does.

A list of your accomplishments. After you've told your prospective employer that you did the job, you have to demonstrate that you were *good* at it. (After all, you're not going to be hired just because you showed up at your last job!) This is the place where you should be specific. This is one of the few places on your resume where you'll be able to talk about your qualities *quantitatively*—in a way that's objective and easily understood.

What money-saving ideas have you come up with, and how much did they trim expenses? By how much did you or your department exceed goals? These are accomplishments anyone can understand.

5. Education

The facts about your academic life generally follow the section about your experience. However, as we've mentioned, there are several circumstances in which the details of your student life should precede the experience section:

1. If you are a recent or soon-to-be college graduate, you should list your academic credentials before any descriptions of internships and other temporary or noncareer-oriented work.
2. If you are changing careers and your education is more pertinent to your prospective new position than your actual job experience.
3. If you're seeking a job in which specialized education is a prerequisite for employment.

In putting together this section of your resume, provide only the basic details about your education—unless of course this is the only selling point you have. The resume should show:

1. Name and location of the school.
2. Date of graduation.
3. Your degree and major area of study. (You can use the abbreviated terms for your degree, such as B.A., B.S., etc.)
4. Your grade point average (optional).
5. Relevant and/or noteworthy awards and accomplishments.

The order in which you present this material depends on the points you wish to emphasize most. If you graduated from a very prestigious school, place the name of the school first, then your degree.

If you didn't graduate college, does that mean you should throw all of the work you did at school out the window? Of course not! State the years you attended and the credit hours you completed. If you completed a large number of hours in a particular field of study, say so. For instance:

Jasper Johns School of Visual Arts, 42 credits in commercial design courses, 1988-1991.

How true to your school?

Even if high school was one of the best times in your life, you shouldn't include this information on your resume unless you did *not* attend college or trade school.

If you were a high school dropout, but earned an equivalency degree, include that on your resume instead. If you moved around a lot during your high school years, list only the last school attended and from which you received your diploma. Include the same types of information you would for a college degree, except for area of study.

If you've been in the work force for a number of years, you needn't include the name of your high school at all. Employers will be more interested in your job experience than in any secondary schooling you might have had.

The GPA option

It's not necessary to include your grade point average if you've been in the work force for several years. The accomplishments and experience you describe on the resume should be enough to indicate to a prospective employer that you are intelligent and hardworking. If you showed true signs of genius in college, however, include information on your resume indicating this.

A good rule of thumb, no matter how long you've been in the work force, is to show an employer your grades only if they're good enough to be proud of—a B-plus average or better. If your class ranking is impressive (top 10 percent) you might mention that or the fact that you graduated with honors. Don't use overkill in establishing your academic prowess. So, your college line might look like any of these:

B.S., Massachusetts Institute of Technology, Cambridge, Mass., 1987. 3.8/4.0 GPA.

B.A., St. Mary of the Plains, Casper, Wyoming, 1990. Ranked third in class of 320.

L.L.M., New York Law School, 1988. Ranked in top 10% of class.

Above and beyond

If you've had any extraordinary educational experiences—foreign exchange, a seminar course with a very famous professor, a research assistant position—by all means include them on the resume to demonstrate that you are someone who goes beyond the ordinary, accepts new and unusual challenge and has been recognized for excellence.

B.A., English, Babcock College, Lincoln, Nebraska, 1985.

Participated in seminar course given by E.L. Doctorow.

One year of foreign study at Birmingham (England) University.

6. Licensing, special training, certification

List any special training you've had and any professional licenses or certification you currently hold, using the most appropriate headline: "Training and Certification," "Professional Licenses," "Special Training," etc. If you prefer, you can group this information together with your education rather than creating a separate section for it.

For licenses and certification, provide:

1. Name and type of license.
2. State or states in which it is valid, if appropriate.
3. Date acquired.
4. Number of the license, if appropriate.

For instance:

New York City Teaching Certification, special education, 1990.

New Mexico Real Estate License, 1975.

Certified Public Accountant, Alaska, 1988.

New Jersey Plumber's License 2386.

For special training, include:

1. Name of the course.
2. Name and location of the institution where you took the course.
3. Date you completed the training.

If you've had special training as part of your job experience—not run-of-the-mill seminars, but extensive programs—by all means include them on your resume. This information can be presented like this:

Special Training
Telephone Central Office Design: Completed intensive, three-month training program, New Jersey Bell Research Center, Newark, N.J., June 1989.

7. Memberships and activities

The affiliations you mention here might not have anything to do with your career, but they will show prospective employers that you are a well-rounded person capable of managing your time and taking on extra assignments.

The title you give this section should reflect its entire content. If it's a mixed bag, call it simply, "Memberships and Outside Activities." If your extracurricular activities are fairly specialized, call the section, "Professional Affiliation" or "Community Activities" to reflect that.

In this section, you should include only the organizations in which you are *now* involved. (Remember, this is not a section in which you are trying to provide experiences that will be deemed relevant to the job you're going after.)

These listings should be as brief as possible, providing only the organization name and positions of leadership you've held.

Again, it's probably a good idea not to include any controversial affiliations you might have unless, of course, they support the prospective employer's position on an issue. For instance, if you are an animal-rights activist, it won't hurt to mention that if you are seeking a position with a cosmetics company that prints "No Animal Testing" on its labels.

It's not necessary to include the location of the organization unless it is relatively obscure.

These listings should look something like this:

Fund raiser, March of Dimes, Bucks County Chapter

President, Susquatch Parent Teacher Association

If you've had many *significant* accomplishments as part of your "free-time" activities, you might want to construct or include them in a "Volunteer Activities" section rather than lengthening what is usually a brief section of the resume.

8. Awards and honors

Awards and honors received as a result of your work experience should already have been included within your experience profile. After all, why would you want to include items that speak so well of you here, near the very end of the resume?

If, indeed, you still have significant recognitions to talk about, then list them as "Awards and Honors" or "Additional Honors and Awards" (to flag the resume reviewer to look for others under your "Accomplishments or Experience" section.)

You should provide the name of the award, the organization presenting it and the year in which you received it. Again, don't overdo this section. Include only awards of *significance*.

Outstanding Contribution Award, Glen Ridge Congregational Church, Glen Ridge, N.H., 1990.

Harold H. McGlinchy Award, Outstanding Performance, Montclair Theater, Montclair, N.H., 1992.

9. Hobbies and outside interests

If you can't resist including this section—despite all of the nasty things we said about it in Chapter 2, then please keep it short and simple. Try to list hobbies that employers will perceive as benefits to them. For instance, if you are applying for an interior design job, it might help if one of your hobbies is carpentry.

The Functional Resume

Most parts of a functional resume should be treated in the same manner they are in the chronological version, with the obvious exceptions of work experience and accomplishments. Here are the basics:

Skill and experience profile

As discussed in Chapter 3, the big difference between chronological and functional resumes is that instead of listing each position you've held, along with its accomplishments and responsibilities, you will divide your experience into general areas of skill and briefly state the experience, qualifications and accomplishments related to each of these areas.

Think about the skills you wish to highlight, taking into careful consideration what the prospective employer needs for the position you will be seeking.

For example, suppose you're applying for a job as a supervisor at a day-care center. What general areas of expertise would be most important? Childcare, teaching, management and general business.

Ideally, of course, you would have at least some experience, qualifications and accomplishments to list in each of these areas. That experience might come from a combination of paid jobs, volunteer positions and in-the-home responsibilities.

Under each skills category heading, you should list four or five of your most impressive accomplishments or abilities. For instance:

Childcare Experience

- Provided in-home day care for three preschoolers for two years.
- Assisted with toddler care in corporate day-care center.
- Developed "child file" system that made vital medical data on day-care children easier to access and maintain.
- Raised three children.

Management Experience

- Supervised three cashiers as first-line supervisor in large discount store.
- Created employee scheduling procedure that resolved long-standing staffing conflict.
- Named Employee of the Month for designing and implementing improved inventory return system.
- Coordinated and directed activities of 100 PTA volunteers for annual fund-raising dinner for three years.

How'd it turn out?

Whether you've been burning to write your resume or dreading it, you probably have a good idea about what to say.

The best thing to do is relax. Remember that this is your first draft, a document that *should* be subjected to several revisions. So, just follow the basic rules of thumb in this and the preceding chapters, and let it flow.

Then, when you're happy with the way it sounds, read the next chapters to get a good feel for how it should look.

Chapter 5

Good Looks Are *Everything*

It is a bit frightening that it's so easy to throw most resumes away without a second look. Think about what the unfortunate candidates would do if they could see the screening process. They'd be screaming, "Hey, wait a minute. That's my life on that piece of paper you just deep-sixed!"

Our answer to many of these hapless candidates would be, "You should have thought about that before sending us this poorly written, poorly presented mess."

In the previous four chapters, we've dealt with format and writing style extensively. In this chapter we will talk about the first impression your resume makes—the picture of *you* it conveys as the recruiter or prospective employer simply looks at it.

The four hallmarks of a well-designed resume are:

1. It's easy to read.
2. There is lots of white space.
3. It's neat.
4. It's clean.

Send an employer a resume that obeys those four rules, and it will get at least more than a glance.

Let's talk about each of these points a bit.

Easy to read

The resume presentation should be simple and uncluttered. While it shouldn't say "RESUME" at the top, its very look should communicate that it is, indeed, a resume.

In order to be easily read, it should have sufficiently large type, should be on white or cream stock and should have a consistent presentation style.

Lots of white space

We've talked about how jam-packed with information your resume must be in the first four chapters of this book. By urging you to have lots of space, are we contradicting ourselves?

No. In order for your readers to read your resume, they must feel *invited* to do so. Graphic designers speak about "entry points" on a page and "places for the eye to rest." Such points and places are sufficiently wide margins, spacing between paragraphs and the space around headlines.

A crammed, cramped resume is forbidding to the reader. At least subconsciously it suggests that there's too much to read and that understanding the resume will be difficult. It also suggests that the resume writer could not decide what to leave out of the resume to give it a cleaner look. And no employer wants to hire indecisive candidates.

Neatness, cleanliness count

Have your resume professionally typeset or output on a laser printer. These are the *only* acceptable ways to have resumes reproduced. Photocopies, typewritten pages and other such products are not acceptable. They will look second rate to any recruiter.

Yes, we've seen resumes with stains, resumes that have obviously been folded after someone just finished reading an over-inked edition of the morning paper, resumes in fairly beaten-up envelopes. What does this say about these candidates? Nothing flattering.

Don't be a slob when it comes to job hunting. Take the extra time—a matter of minutes really—to put your best foot forward in a well-polished shoe.

12 tips for better-looking resumes

1. Use a serif typeface. Serif typefaces, such as New Century Schoolbook used in this book, are easy on the eye. Serif typefaces are those that have extra strokes on the letters. For some reason, tests always show that people find many of these typefaces easier to read. Open any textbook, magazine, newspaper or turn on your word processor and you'll see serif type. We see many resumes that have sans-serif typefaces—those lacking those finials and doodads that mark the serif faces—and, we can tell you, they are harder to read.

2. But don't get too fancy. Stick to traditional-looking typefaces. You may love the sound of Old English Text or Zapf Chancery Italic, but it won't look as good on your resume as Times Roman.

3. Choose a face and stick to it. Leave the mixing of various type styles to trained graphic artists. When amateurs mix typefaces on a single document, the results are usually, well, amateurish.

4. Make sure the type is big enough, but not too big. The standard size is usually 10-"point" type, with a similar size of "leading" or space between the lines. If asked, you would say 10 over 10 New Century Schoolbook; 10-point type size and 10 points of leading between the lines.

5. Highlight with boldface type. While you shouldn't mix typefaces, you can make certain items—such as your name, the names of organizations, employers and schools, and headlines stand out by using boldface (or very dark) versions of the same typeface.

6. Use underlining and capitalization of entire words and phrases sparingly. At most, use such treatment on section heads. Such jarring changes of style slow a reader's eye.

7. The same goes for italics. Again, you shouldn't mix type styles too much at all. Also, your goal is to emphasize everything in your resume through punchy writing and proper positioning, so italics for the sake of emphasis are redundant.

8. Don't skimp on the margins. You should have a frame of at least one inch of white space on the top and no less than one-half inch on the other three sides of your resume. Narrow margins will make your document look "choked."

9. Use "ragged right" line breaks. This means your lines should end naturally, not requiring words to be hyphenated. This will provide for more white space than the box-like "justified" line endings you see in most books.

10. Use single line spacing within listings, double spacing between sections and paragraphs.

11. Use bullets to highlight accomplishments, but limit the size of bulleted items to one to two lines. Bullets help you deliver a large number of selling points in a crisp, telegraph-like style. Using lengthy bulleted paragraphs, therefore, will only assure that your resume shoots blanks.

12. Keep it simple. Once you find a presentation style you like, stick with it. Don't overdesign your resume or try to include every presentation style you've liked. Find the one you like best and use it throughout the document.

The second part of this book presents a wide variety of resume formats. Find one that you like and try it, keeping in mind the rules we've delivered here.

Chapter 6

The Art of Editing and Rewriting

Ernest Hemingway delivered what is probably the best advice on how to write effectively: "I write standing up and edit sitting down." What he meant by that was: You should spend more time editing—changing and deleting—than you do writing.

Edit, edit and edit some more

Let's suppose you've written a rough draft of your resume. How do you go about making it better, even if you already think it's pretty darn good? First, look at the big changes you might have to make. Make them. And then take a look at the details and see how those can be corrected or improved.

The big picture

Here are some questions to ask yourself that might lead to major overhauls of your first crack at a resume masterpiece:

1. Have I communicated to the employer that I can fill a *need*? If your resume reads like an autobiography or a series of job descriptions and yearbook entries, you've missed the boat.

Ask yourself: Does this resume tell the employer what I can do for him or her? Does it make him or her confident that I am qualified and motivated enough to be given a chance? Have I spelled out the many benefits the employer would realize by hiring me?

2. Do my strengths come across? Have I chosen a format that highlights my pluses and does not suggest skeletons in the closet? Will the functional format make it seem as if I have something to hide? Will the chronological format make it look as if I'm a hopeless job-hopper?

3. Is there anything that can be removed? Does the list of volunteer activities suggest qualities that would be useful to the employer, or is it a meaningless list of names and dates? What does my list of hobbies really say about me? Have I accomplished enough in my career to have a summary of qualifications?

4. Does every element count? Is the job objective meaningful or does it sound as exciting as accounting-textbook prose? Did I put my best foot forward in the skills summary? Are all of the elements crisp and compelling?

Details, details, details

Once you have a resume that you're happy with and that meets the standards suggested by these questions, it's time to get out the magnifying glass and check that all of the details are right.

Here's a checklist that will help you through this editing process.

Name header

- ❑ Are my name, address and phone number prominently displayed at the top of the page?
- ❑ Did I use the most professional-sounding version of my name? (Frances instead of Cookie? William instead of Billy?)
- ❑ Did I include my address, and is it correct? If I am going to be moving, did I indicate my future address and the date after which I can be found there?
- ❑ Did I include a phone number at which I can be easily reached or at which a message can be left? Did I include my area code? (Check and double-check that numbers haven't been transposed—a common mistake.)

Job objective

- ❑ Have I stated the objective in 12 or fewer words?
- ❑ Is it focused and precise?
- ❑ Does it preclude my being considered for other positions? If so, should I draft alternative versions of my resume, each with a different objective?

Skills summary

- ❑ Is it targeted to the job I'm seeking? Does it highlight the qualifications and experience that are most important to my prospective employer?
- ❑ Is it short and concise—two to three brief sentences or four or five bulleted points?

Experience profile for the chronological resume

- ❑ Did I include the correct starting and ending dates (month and year) for each job?
- ❑ Did I use the correct job title or a revised title in keeping with my actual duties and responsibilities?
- ❑ Did I include the correct name of my various employers and the locations in which I worked?
- ❑ Are any of the paragraphs I've used to describe my jobs longer than five lines?

Functional and combination resumes

- ❑ Are the skill categories the most relevant to the job I want?
- ❑ Did I use business-oriented terms for skill category headings ("Childcare" rather than "Baby-sitting")?

- ❑ Did I include a brief chronological listing of paid and volunteer experience toward the end of the resume?

All formats

- ❑ Did I use strong action words to describe my contribution or achievements? (Review the list of verbs on page 36.)
- ❑ Did I eliminate "I," "the," "an" and other words unnecessary in resume writing?
- ❑ Did I use acronyms or abbreviations that might not be understood by everyone who will look at my resume?
- ❑ Did I *quantify* my accomplishments, rather than simply describe them? Did I talk about the amount of money I saved or by what percentage I increased sales?
- ❑ Did I use the correct name for each award and honor received? Did I state the organization that gave it and the year in which it was received?

Education

- ❑ Did I check the dates I received my degrees or attended schools?
- ❑ Did I include the name and location of each school?

Proofread again...and again

One typo can land your resume in the trash. So, why blow a job because of a transposed letter or a stupid misspelling?

Proofreading is impossible to teach, but we can give you some pointers:

1. Get out a ruler and read each and every line of your resume. This will force you to *slow down* your reading.
2. Don't rely solely on a spell-checker program. Such computer aids don't recognize the difference between "their" and "there" and "its" and "it's." So, run the spell-checker to catch spelling mistakes, but check it the old-fashioned way once it's output to look for other types of errors.
3. Read from the bottom up. Often, we tend to read faster when we're reading for sense. So, make sure the resume won't make any sense by reading it from the lower right-hand corner backwards.
4. Don't go it alone. It's difficult to catch all of the errors in something you've pored over for hours or days. Have someone with "fresh eyes" give your final draft a careful read.

After you've proofread the resume, make corrections and check it again, making sure the resume is no less than perfect.

Now you know the basics, including content, format and design, of how to put together a great resume.

It's time to turn to the second part of this book, in which we're proud to present the resumes deemed "The Best I've Ever Seen" by some of the leading experts in the career field.

RESUMES! RESUMES! RESUMES!

What, Me Worry About Finding a Job?

A Question of Balance

"This resume is effective because it unveils the candidate much the way a good newspaper story does," notes the staff of AIM Executive, the human resources consulting firm that submitted this example from Alfred E. Neuman. "It has a great lead, encapsulating what is to come, followed by more specific development of the story."

For each of his past positions, Neuman takes pains to describe his overall job responsibilities. "In addition, he demonstrates his level of performance in a few hard-hitting achievement statements that quickly get the message across," notes AIM.

Especially impressive here is the use of numbers that lend a great deal of credibility to the candidate's statement of his credentials. He "improved on-time delivery from 47% to 89%..." and "achieved 3-day response time on all orders to key customers..."

"This makes a strong case that the candidate has a record of high performance," notes AIM.

In addition, AIM was particularly impressed by the look of this resume. "The presentation makes balanced use of fonts, there is a good spatial relationship between paragraphs and bulleted statements and sufficient white space facilitates quick scanning."

AIM Executive, Inc.

AIM Executive, Inc., founded in 1977, is a diversified human resources consulting firm dedicated to helping clients achieve their organizational objectives. As one of the fastest-growing privately held companies in America, AIM Executive was included on *INC.* magazine's prestigious *INC.* 500 list for four consecutive years. AIM Executive offers outplacement services throughout the U.S. and overseas in all major industrial sectors.

ALFRED E. NEUMAN

1000 Homerun Drive
Mountain, Colorado 80020

303-543-1234/*Home* 303-543-2345/*Office*

CAREER OBJECTIVE

A senior level position directing manufacturing operations in a corporation desiring organizational transformation.

PROFILE

Results-oriented manufacturing professional with proven track record of producing significant operational improvements in on-time delivery, quality of managing systems as well as products, reduced inventories, increased productivity and cost reductions that have positively impacted bottom-line results. Strategic thinker and visionary leader who models a purposeful, pro-active approach that builds organizational capability to focus on fire prevention rather than fire fighting. A people-oriented team player who is committed to creating an open, trustful environment to achieve positive change through effective employee empowerment.

PROFESSIONAL EXPERIENCE

OUTDOOR PRODUCTS COMPANY, Denver, CO 1991 to 1992

Vice President - Operations

Managed 500+ employee, multi-plant operations of $100MM juvenile products division of major recreational products corporation. Supplied the highly-competitive, fast-paced mass retailer market with innovative products that were produced directly in proprietary, high-volume, repetitive manufacturing plants or procured from foreign-based sources. Directly responsible for manufacturing, quality assurance, material planning and control, domestic and foreign purchasing, engineering and distribution.

- **Improved on-time delivery from 47% to 89% through implementation of demand flow/just-in-time manufacturing processes.**
- **Achieved 3-day response time on all orders to key customer while improving inventory turns from 6.2 to 7.4.**
- **Led strategic planning process to transform company toward world class manufacturing status.**

STUFF MANUFACTURING CO., Downs, KY 1989 to 1991

Plant Manager

Responsible for operations at $25MM unionized metal fabrication plant and remote customer service/distribution center that manufactured office accessories. Operation was division of $200MM arts and crafts/office products corporation.

- **Improved customer service to 90% line fill within 5 days while reducing FGI by over 25%.**
- **Reduced response time for supplying replacement parts to customers from over 7 days to next day shipment.**

TOWNE MICROWAVE, INC., Towne, OH 1986 to 1988

Director of Operations

Responsible for manufacturing and all directly related support functions in non-union plant of $100MM consumer electronics company which manufactured and direct marketed *Escort*, *Passport*, and *Solo* radar detectors.

- **Increased productivity 16% (from 7.3 to 8.5 units per person per day).**
- **Directed the design of a Total Quality Assurance program which improved first time yields from 60% to above 90%.**
- **Revised material schedule and control procedures reducing in-process inventory from 8 days to 3 days and total inventory from over $7MM to under $5MM.**

IN-LINE ENGINE COMPANY 1973 to 1985

Director - Assembly and Test, Rocky Road, NC (1980-1985)

Directed design, start-up and operation of engine assembly segment of state-of-the-art, $350MM, 1.1 million square feet diesel engine manufacturing plant. Responsible for engine assembly, test, paint and shipping operations plus related support functions.

- **Accomplished start-up on time and 10% below budget despite a 9-month schedule compression.**
- **Mobilized all plant personnel to produce 400 engines per week (150% of previous best performance) 5 months after start-up to get current with orderboard.**
- **Created self-directed work teams within innovative structure of business units which operated as semi-autonomous mini-plants within the plant. Operation was non-union.**

Manager - Assembly, Johns, NY (1976-1980)

Responsible for planning, start-up and operation of engine assembly line with innovative, team-based organization. Managed staff of 5 team advisors, 7 professional resources, and 90 non-exempt employees in non-union environment.

- **Developed self-directed, multi-skilled work teams which became a model for organizational development at other In-Line entities.**
- **Achieved start-up on time and under budget. Met production goal 15 consecutive months after start-up with quality and delivery performance superior to sister plants.**

Various Management Assignments, Columbus, OH (1973-1976)

EDUCATION

MBA, Indiana University, Bloomington, IN
BS, Metallurgical Engineering, Purdue University

Power Resume Tip

Your resume should *never* be handwritten, written in calligraphy, mimeographed, copied on a Ditto machine or duplicated by carbon paper.

A Resume That Achieved Great Results

"A .300 Batting Average"

"This resume for a chemical marketing professional generated a response rate of 30 percent when it was used to answer employment ads," notes Charles F. Albrecht, president of the Eastern Division for Drake Beam Morin, Inc., the world's largest career consulting firm. "The one-paragraph summary begins by highlighting three major areas of success," points out Albrecht. He says that this number is just right. "One accomplishment area would make the resume too limiting. Seven or eight might communicate lack of focus or cause the reader to believe that the candidate is exaggerating his accomplishments."

Albrecht notes that "throughout the resume, the candidate backs up his statement in the Summary that he is a results-oriented, self-motivated, award-winning marketing professional. For instance, he was a three-time award winner in one environment and had a success ratio 2.5 times the company average in another."

In addition, this candidate's career progression is nicely highlighted. "The most impressive and greatest number of accomplishments are listed under the most recent position. And the candidate did not waste valuable space with early accomplishments in an entry-level position." Albrecht also points out that the candidate's accomplishment statements are "full of qualifiers: actual amounts of sales and revenue increases, cost savings and time frames. The candidate projects an image of a person who gets quantifiable results quickly."

And this resume did the same!

Charles F. Albrecht, Jr.
President, Eastern Division, Drake Beam Morin, Inc.

Drake Beam Morin, Inc. is the world's largest career consulting firm, with more than 100 U.S. and international offices and assisting over 200,000 candidates each year in the construction of their resumes. Charles F. Albrecht, Jr., is responsible for DBM's operations and sales in the Eastern U.S. and DBM's Key Account Program.

RYAN M. FOYT
1234 Lake Avenue
Ringwood, NJ 07456
201-555-7626

SUMMARY

Twelve years of diversified experience and success in sales, marketing and technical service with a technical background in chemistry. Results-oriented, self-motivated, award-winning marketing professional.

Strengths include:

- Direct Sales
- Market/Product Analysis
- Project Management
- Strategy Development
- Troubleshooting
- Quality Management
- Program Administration
- Personal Computer Skills

EXPERIENCE

THE MIDWEST CHEMICAL COMPANY, Chicago, IL 1986-1991

Senior Marketing Representative

Represented company in technical sales and marketing for new business venture. Responsible for development and implementation of marketing strategies and programs.

- Conceived, developed and administered several advertising, distributor and sales support programs, resulting in sales increase from $140M to $1.2MM.
- Created, as member of special task force, initial strategic business plan leading to the acquisition of $30MM company.
- Sold and managed comprehensive maintenance savings project for client company, resulting over a three-year period in savings of $500M to client and revenues of $300M to Midwest Chemical.
- Within twelve-week period, managed launch of new product line, including generation of product inventory and literature.
- Coordinated annual three-day training seminar leading to signing of $400M per year distributor.
- Reduced out-of-stock complaints 90% by conceiving, programming and instituting a LOTUS 1-2-3 spreadsheet program to guide manufacturing planning.

RAYMOND TECHNICAL, INC., Newark, DE 1985-1986

Marketing Representative

Marketed and developed business for $7MM, 140 member consulting and engineering firm specializing in structural, chemical, environmental engineering and construction management.

- Proposed and conducted marketing research project identifying top growth markets and local area prospects.
- Planned and performed business development campaign resulting in success ratio 2.5 times company average, achieving $1.7MM in revenues from 17 successful projects.

HARRIS SERVICE & SUPPLIES, INC., Philadelphia, PA 1984-1985

Technical Sales Engineer

Designed, specified and sold custom-designed state-of-the-art systems, primarily to biomedical market.

- Proposed and sold $250M of equipment and service contracts, increasing sales by 30%.

ESSEX WATER, Philadelphia, PA 1981-1984

Accounts Manager

Managed 110 accounts in three-county, $300M territory. Supplied technical advice and support on industrial water treatment programs.

- Increased sales by 10% per year. Three-time award winner for top salesperson of quarter.

DCM, Pittsburgh, PA 1978-1981

Field Representative

Supplied lab and field chemistry support and training for water treatment accounts.

EDUCATION

B.S., Chemistry—University of Pittsburgh—1978
Computer Programming Minor

Power Resume Tip

Make sure your resume is neat, clean and easy to read. Type and white space should be arranged so that the reader's eye is drawn quickly from beginning to end.

The Creation of a Successful Marketing Tool

Ten Steps to a Winning Resume

"When you are developing a resume, the primary goal is the creation of a successful marketing tool that showcases the client's selling points to the potential 'buyer,' " says Vicki Bacal, president of The Resume Specialist in Minneapolis. Carol Kingsley's resume illustrates Bacal's basic rules quite well. The resume should:

1. Address the needs of the reader, answering the question, "Why should I hire you?" Note Kingsley's "demonstrated history of success."
2. Highlight outstanding characteristics in a rapid-fire Summary of Qualifications to provide a quick overview. Note use of "resourceful problem-solver."
3. Tell the reader *how you made a difference*. Note Kingsley's "producing over $3 million in sales."
4. Be clear, concise and specific. Use facts and figures to add credibility.
5. Emphasize your key accomplishments with short sentences and descriptive action verbs to gain and hold reader attention. Note Kingsley's use of "performed as primary resource."
6. Use repetition of key ideas to remind the reader of your greatest strengths and achievements. Note repetition of "identifying," "customer relations" and "meeting needs."
7. Let the reader know that you understand the industry by using insider terminology. Note use of "point of sale report" and "network tracking."
8. Use attractive graphics, white space, underlining and boldface to draw reader interest. Short lines are also important for readability.
9. Highlight on-the-job and continuing education to emphasize current knowledge and augment undergraduate education.
10. Take credit for your role in successful projects. Note Kingsley's many examples of initiative and accomplishment.

Vicki Bacal, M.A.
The Resume Specialist

Vicki Bacal has advised more than 8,000 clients nationwide since 1985 in the areas of resume writing, interview preparation and job search strategy. With a background in public relations and higher education, she brings a marketing-oriented approach to client projects. A frequent speaker and seminar leader, Bacal is presently a career consultant to the Women's Employment and Resource Center in Minneapolis. She is an active member of the Twin Cities-based Resume Network.

1049 Tapestry Avenue South
New Brighton, MN 55447

Carol Kingsley

Residence: 612 555-9433
Office: 612 555-3394

SUMMARY of PROFESSIONAL QUALIFICATIONS

- ❑ Experienced Sales Professional with demonstrated history of success.
- ❑ Highly effective in communication and customer relations.
- ❑ Resourceful problem-solver, skilled in identifying and meeting needs.
- ❑ Able to work well independently and achieve objectives.
- ❑ Quick study; welcomes new challenges.

EXPERIENCE

CHEOPS INTERNATIONAL, St. Paul, MN
Designers/manufacturers of IBM compatible computers; annual sales $250MM+.
Account Manager, 1991 to Present

- Generate high sales volume of PC hardware and related products to Fortune 500 corporations and small businesses nationwide, producing over $3 million in sales.
- Establish and develop positive customer relations through immediate follow up, product knowledge and exceptional service, resulting in strong client loyalty and repeat business.
- Effectively manage new accounts, identifying and meeting client needs.
- Actively initiate new business through written and verbal communication.

SEAGATE TECHNOLOGY, INC., Minnetonka, MN
Formerly IMPRIMIS TECHNOLOGY.
Sales Specialist, with extensive travel nationwide, 1990

- Interacted effectively with senior management, production managers and sales force to implement reseller and distribution strategies.
- Created successful sales promotions and incentives to expand business.

IMPRIMIS TECHNOLOGY, Minnetonka, MN
A wholly owned subsidiary of CONTROL DATA CORPORATION.
International Sales Consultant, 1989

- Organized and implemented a successful International Distributor Forum.
- Conceived and developed innovative corporate communication tools for domestic and international customers.

CONTROL DATA CORPORATION, Bloomington, MN
Customer Relations Representative – HEADQUARTERS, 1987 to 1989

- Performed as primary resource to all national distributors/sales force.
- Provided product training at the industry's largest computer exposition.

Sales Administrator – DATA PRODUCTS GROUP, 1983 to 1987

- Co-developed the company's first point-of-sale report for network tracking.

CONTINUING PROFESSIONAL EDUCATION

CHEOPS Sales Training Program

- **New Product Training**
- **Sales Strategies**
- **Solution Selling**

CONTROL DATA Sales Training Program

- **Basic Sales Techniques**
- **Customer Relations**
- **Computer Software Applications**

EDUCATION

AUGSBURG COLLEGE, Minneapolis, MN
Liberal Arts Program, in progress.

MINNEAPOLIS BUSINESS COLLEGE, Minneapolis, MN
Business Communications coursework.

A Long List In a Little Space

"King of the One-Liners"

The most impressive thing about Peter Blue's resume is that it says so much in a relatively small amount of space. It does this by allotting one line—and one line only—to each of a long list of accomplishments. "Writing one-line thoughts requires great discipline and really enforces economy of language," says Howard Bennett, senior campaign manager for Power Marketing, an outplacement firm based in San Francisco, "but it has great impact on the reader."

Bennett notes that Blue's resume is a good illustration of some other basic resume rules he advises:

1. Use the chronological format. *Never* write a functional resume—headhunters and corporate employment managers regard them as "problem" resumes and are suspicious of candidates who use them.
2. One, two and even three page resumes are okay, depending upon your background and length of tenure. If you have 10 or more years of significant achievements, don't shortchange yourself by trying to stick to one page. Just be sure to sell yourself on the first page.
3. Put a clear, targeted objective at the top—the very best kind is a job title or professional title. Then support the objective with a brief qualifications summary that features your important selling points.
4. When writing about your experience, *quantify everything*. Give names, numbers and definitions—all of these add to your credibility.
5. Don't miss the opportunity to demonstrate your promotions within an organization.
6. Demonstrate your skills by telling stories—describe major projects that showcase your talents and separate you from the competition. Be sure to list bottom-line achievements.
7. Leave lots of white space and use bullets, underlining and bold type for emphasis, but don't overdo graphics. Employ nonjustified type and "gaze motion" (smooth curves on the right margin of paragraphs) so that the eye moves comfortably down the page.

Howard Bennett

Senior Campaign Manager, Power Marketing

Power Marketing, a San Francisco-based corporate outplacement firm, has brought a pragmatic, marketing-based approach to the job search. Power Marketing uses the same brand management techniques in the job market that Procter & Gamble uses to sell consumer products. Its methods have achieved results (in the form of new jobs) for candidates ranging from plant workers to $1 million-a-year CEOs.

PETER BLUE
1234 56th Avenue
San Francisco, CA 94567
415-555-4567

MANAGER OF LOGISTICS & DISTRIBUTION

QUALIFICATIONS
- BBA-Personnel Management, 20 years in distribution management
- Specialist in work and manpower planning and quality improvement
- Experience in inventory control software development and application
- Background in hazardous materials storage, transportation, disposal

---

PROFESSIONAL EXPERIENCE

ABC Scientific, Inc., Colma, CA 1987 to Present
REGIONAL WAREHOUSE MANAGER

- **Manage warehouse for $600 million international scientific products distributor.** Responsible for western region including California, Washington and Pacific Rim. Administer $3.2MM operating budget, report to Regional Distribution Manager. Direct six supervisors, 60 union warehousepersons and six support staff.
- **Responsible for $13MM inventory, 80,000 line items, 230,000 sq. ft. warehouse.** Manage receiving, checking, picking, packing and shipping of 1,500 orders daily. Operate facility in compliance with OSHA and DOT standards.
- **Distribute scientific, laboratory, photographic supplies and equipment.** Products and equipment include chemicals, hazardous materials, lab furniture, diagnostic instruments, cleanroom and lab supplies, refrigerated and sterile items.
- **Serve clients in education, biotechnology, soil testing and water treatment** industries including Syntex, UCSF, UCLA, Stanford, Kodak, Amgen, IBM, CH2M Hill. Work with 900 manufacturers including Nalge, Corning Glass, JT Baker, EM Science.

Major Projects

- **Established procedures for hazardous material storage and disposal.** Developed and implemented hazardous material stock rotation plan. Conducted hazardous material/safety training for employees.
- **Developed and implemented performance and quality improvement program.** Redefined warehouse positions, established hourly production standards.
- **Streamlined inventory identification and tracking system.** Introduced systematic analysis of daily discrepancy reports. Standardized receiving, stocking, checking and housekeeping procedures.

Achievements

* Saved 10% in packing costs by recycling and use of alternative packing materials.
* Reduced inventory discrepancies 45% annually by developing tracking system.
* Cut disposal of hazardous materials 50% by implementing storage procedures.
* Increased employee productivity 15% by establishing production standards.
* Reduced injury claims 40% by introducing safety awareness program.
* Consistently met 24-hour turnaround goal for 93% of shipments.
* Reduced breakage 80% by designing new product packaging.

Continued....

PROFESSIONAL EXPERIENCE (Continued)

XYZ Tire Company, Chicago/Reno 1970 to 1987
DISTRIBUTION MANAGER (1985 to 1987)

- **Managed 425,000 sq. ft. warehouse for $2 billion rubber products manufacturer.** Responsible for $15MM, 500,000-unit tire inventory and public warehouse operation. Supervised ten administrative staff, directed 45 contract warehousepersons. Managed $2MM budget, reported to National Distribution Manager.
- **Supervised receiving, inventory control, storage, security, distribution, traffic.** Scheduled drivers, negotiated rates and routes with truck lines/carriers.
- **Managed product distribution, security and receivables for 24 public accounts.** Inventory included appliances, chemicals, hospital supplies, electronic products.

Major Projects/Achievements
* Increased productivity 10% by application of WOFAC-based computerized systems.
* Increased storage capacity 10% by standardizing inventory control procedures.
* Developed operations manual and cross-training plan for six job functions.
* Upgraded warehouse output from lowest in company ranking to second.
* Implemented special security procedures for public accountants.

ASSISTANT DISTRIBUTION MANAGER (1976 to 1985)

- **Responsible for warehouse administration of 200,000 sq. ft. facility.** Received and shipped 20,000 tires daily to 11 western states and Pacific Rim. Managed receiving, storage and shipping of $7 million tire inventory. Supervised 50 warehousepersons and data processing staff.

Major Projects/Achievements
* Increased productivity over 15% through WOFAC work measurement program.
* Consulted to four regional facilities to improve manpower planning.
* Designed and wrote audit approved cycle inventory procedures.
* Established personnel policies and procedures.

WAREHOUSE SUPERVISOR (1974 to 1976)

- **Supervised 100,000 sq. ft. facility with $5 million inventory.** Inventory included tires, footwear, industrial products, auto/home supplies.

WAREHOUSE FOREMAN (1970 to 1974)

- **Responsible for receiving, storage, shipping, order entry and customer service.** Supervised 22 union warehousepersons and 16 support staff.
  * Joined company as Order Entry Clerk; promoted to Foreman after two years.

EDUCATION BBA, Personnel Management, Northwestern University, Chicago, 1977
Completed 15 MBA units, University of Nevada, Las Vegas, 1985

PROFESSIONAL Completed courses/seminars in hazardous waste, transportation, traffic, safety, employee involvement and leadership

TECHNICAL IBM Mainframe, DEC 1050, BASIC

Power Resume Tip

Use bullets or asterisks to highlight accomplishments or explanatory phrases. This not only breaks up a lot of information into bite-size portions, but also helps pull out key selling points that would be buried if presented in long paragraph form.

Bottom Line: It's Interesting

A Very Different, But Effective, Format

Here is a resume that's definitely not for the faint of heart. Its format and language are quite out of the ordinary right from the beginning. Where are the candidate's address and phone number? Where are the familiar headings such as "Experience" and "Education?" This resume breaks the rules, but it all works quite well, according to S. Michael Boyer, executive vice president of Kobek Boyer & Associates, a marketing consulting firm based in Indianapolis.

"This resume has terrific clarity, appropriateness of information, layout/design, attention to detail and support of accomplishments. It makes me want to know *more* about the candidate. If this individual performs as a Senior Contract Executive similar to the way in which he produces a resume, he should be very successful throughout his career."

The intriguing elements here are the all-lower-case headings to the left, which are written in the style of advertising blurbs. The "other facts" section gives a clear picture of the candidate's personality.

In the text of the resume, this candidate shuns the use of bullets, choosing instead to italicize key elements within the rather long paragraphs. He also uses testimonials right within the text of the document rather effectively.

"Right from the very first line, this resume is concise and to the point," says Boyer. " 'Senior Contract Executive' unequivocally states the primary qualifications of the candidate. It is immediately followed by his brief career objective, which reinforces the candidate's high level of qualifications.

"The headings to the left entice the reader to continue. The bottom line is, this resume is *interesting*."

The literal bottom line of this resume is a call-to-action similar to that found in effective direct-mail copy. That's where we find out how to contact this individual who certainly has gotten our attention.

S. Michael Boyer

Executive Vice President, Kobek Boyer & Associates, Inc.

Kobek Boyer and Associates, Inc., is an Indianapolis-based marketing consulting firm. Boyer serves as the managing partner of its Human Resource Management Group. This division provides staff recruiting and sales/customer service training to corporate clients. Boyer has nearly 20 years experience planning and directing sales and marketing campaigns, including recruiting and training nearly 4,000 sales and service staff members for a variety of large organizations.

PETER F. TURNER

Senior Contract Executive

objective

Particularly where there is a need for aggressive and innovative acquisition oversight supported by a thorough knowledge of government law, policies, procedures and regulations.

"leading-edge" management results

Developed an acquisition strategy as Director of Contracting to streamline the contracting process, which reduced lead time by 64%. Produced negotiated savings of $3.6 million. Placed $150 million in contracts, concurrent with a 20% reduction in operational budget. Received US Army and Small Business Administration awards for best Small and Disadvantaged business program. Negotiated historical labor agreements with the National Federation of Federal Employees. Selected as premier labor relations executive by president of the union. Selected as Equal Employment Opportunity Manager of the year. (US Army Training Center and Fort Jackson, Fort Jackson, SC, 1987-Present.)

"cradle-to-grave" contract management

Sought and obtained key African and Middle Eastern projects, which served as a critical transition vehicle for my agency to a diversified marketing strategy. Developed and implemented a highly mobile infrastructure of contracting professionals able to respond to short-term highly politically visible projects with no advance notice. Developed and implemented a comprehensive reorganization plan for my agency. Composed the requirements, negotiated and subsequently brought to award $18 million CPAF services contract. Selected as Contracting Officer with $5 million contract signature authority. Conceived and implemented a comprehensive plan for the closeout of politically visible $100 million contract. Uncovered and recouped $1.5 million in unallowable contract costs. (US Army Corps of Engineers, Middle East Division, Berryville, VA 1981-1987)

versatility in contract guidance

Served as Acting Chief, Construction Support Branch in overseas post. Directed the performance evaluation of two multimillion dollar CPAF Service Contracts. Negotiated, promoted and obtained the approval of the Ministry of Defense and Aviation, Saudi Arabia, for $20 million in fixed-price and cost type support contracts. According to supervisor, "...performed all duties in an outstanding manner." (US Army Corps of Engineers, Middle East Division, Riyadh, Saudi Arabia, 1980-1981)

diversity in contract administration

Single-handedly administered 250 CPFF, CPAF and cost contracts within extremely tight fiscal and budgetary constraints. Closed-out 12 CPFF and cost contracts that had lain dormant for two years prior to my arrival. Effected 5%-10% cost in fee reductions through solid, organized negotiation strategies. Rapidly promoted from trainee to functional supervisor of the Contract Administration Branch. "Possesses the enthusiasm, initiative and ability to master any assignment given to him..." was comment received from Chief, Procurement & Supply Office. (US Army Engineer Waterways Experiment Station, Corps of Engineers, Vicksburg, MS, 1977-1980)

education

Master in Public Administration from Harvard University (1986). Interdisciplinary B.S. in criminal justice studies with a minor in accounting. Graduated (1976) 5th in class of 2080 with highest honors at a 3.87 GPA. Served as a resident assistant of a large dormitory, enabling me to pay for every cent of my college education. Vice-President of Phi Kappa Phi scholastic society. Nominated for *Who's Who Among American Colleges and Universities*.

other facts

Born 1954...married...three children...Nominated for President of Harvard class...Served as Vice-Mayor of my residential compound in Saudi Arabia...Top Secret Clearance...Strong ability to lead and motivate subordinate managers...I thrive on challenge and adversity...National Director for the National Contract Management Association (NCMA)...Featured lecturer for NCMA and US Army on leadership, communication and contracting...Certified Professional Contracts Manager (CPCM)

for further details

Telephone (803) 555-4331 (work)...(803) 555-8833 (home)
515 Valley Drive, Columbia, SC 29223

Power Resume Tip

When your resume is completely finished, don't make a single mark on it. Don't pencil in a note, write in an updated phone number or try to cover up an error with correction fluid. The resume you send out must be absolutely flawless.

Compact, With Lots of Power

Effective Use of the Combination Format

This resume packs an incredible amount of punch into one page.

The reviewer will first see an impressive overview of Susan Johnson's career: the Areas of Achievement. A summary such as this gives an up-front here's-what-I-can-do that will tell the potential employer the strengths of the resume writer.

The Employment History provides the details that support the Areas of Achievement. Boldfaced job titles point out the exact work assignments, along with the dates each job was performed.

Extraordinary accomplishments within each job—the ones you want to discuss in the job interview—are italicized to highlight the special mentions of a growing career.

This resume incorporates many of the recommendations that Kathleen Brogan routinely gives to job candidates:

- Less is best. Be as concise as possible.
- Quantify your successes whenever possible.
- Don't drown your readers in an ocean of adjectives.
- Always include a section that summarizes your talents and your experience ("Team Leadership," "Client Service and Relations," etc.)

Kathleen Brogan
Brogan Communications

Kathleen Brogan has been writing resumes, business/personal communications and humorous tributes since 1984. Prior to her writing career, she worked for eight years as a C.P.A. Brogan shares with her customers employment tips, interview strategies, advice and a few great one-liners.

SUSAN M. JOHNSON

31754 Katherine Lane
Suburbia, MN 55888
(612) 123-4567 (voice mail)

AREAS OF ACHIEVEMENT

- Sales Performance
- Written and Verbal Communication
- Marketing Strategies
- Quality Assurance
- Client Service and Relations
- Information/Computer Systems
- Program Development and Implementation
- Team Leadership

EMPLOYMENT HISTORY

BARTZ, ROGERS & PARTNERS, Minnetonka, MN 6/94-Present

Executive Recruiter

- Determine clients' computer/information needs. Provide them candidates for full-time employment and/or short-term projects. Consult clients to discuss candidates' performance.
- Research candidates' backgrounds to determine their level of MIS skills.
- Interview candidates prior to sending them to the client. Assess their current competencies, work preferences, accomplishments, previous employment, and compatibility with clients' work environments.
- ***Secured a large contract resulting in the hire of 130 individuals.***

WEST PUBLISHING CORPORATION, Eagan, MN 5/92 - 6/94

Sales Representative/Promotional Database Writer, 1/94-6/94

- *Selected as the first representative to serve the Canadian market of small law firms.*
- Served as a liaison between product marketers and customers for the development/implementation of attorney listings using a custom-made database.
- Wrote articles featured on Law Firm Marketing Highlights, a database outlining diverse legal trends and technology.

Field Representative, 12/92-12/93

- *Recognized as the first representative to obtain office and attorney information from executives at the world's largest law firm.*
- Marketed and sold West's Legal Directory to the top 500 law firms in an eight state area.
- Developed and expanded exceptional client relations.

Corporate/Government Sales Representative, 5/92-12/92

- *Developed and activated the first lead generation systems for gathering Corporate and Government listings for West's Legal Directory.*
- Added approximately 3,500 new attorney profiles to new databases.
- Worked closely with the executive level decision makers in Fortune 1000 corporations and top government officials at both the state and federal levels.

EAGAN ATHLETIC CLUB, Eagan, MN 5/92-Present

Aerobics Instructor (part-time)

EDUCATION

University of Wisconsin, LaCrosse, WI

Bachelor of Science with emphases in Speech Communication and Sociology 1991

WRITING SAMPLES AND REFERENCES AVAILABLE UPON REQUEST.

Often, Rules Are Meant *Not* to Be Broken

A By-the-Book Resume That Does Its Job Well

"No company ever hired a resume," says Robert W. Caldwell, Jr. "But your resume is important. It is a marketing piece that opens doors to the interview process."

Caldwell, the founder and president of RW Caldwell Associates, Inc., an outplacement firm, says that Bill Larry's resume is good because it answers the three questions all resumes should answer: What do you want to do (objective)? What qualifies you to do it (summary)? How well did you do it in the past (experience and accomplishments)?

The no-nonsense Caldwell argues that an objective is necessary because "it says that you *know* what you want to do and are decisive enough to say so and it saves the reader the task of deciding for you." For instance, Larry's objective is specific but broad enough to attract opportunities.

Caldwell argues that the summary is the resume's "hook," which could help it get more than 30 seconds of the reader's time. "In Bill Larry's summary, note the statement 'Grew company...' That's an attention-getter, the 'hook' that will elicit more than a 30-second reading."

While many recruiters argue against including personal data, Caldwell favors it because it adds "a human touch to an otherwise sterile document."

Robert Caldwell
President, RW Caldwell Associates, Inc.

Robert Caldwell is founder and president of RW Caldwell Associates, Inc., the oldest full-service, corporate-sponsored outplacement firm in western New York. The firm avoids "formula" outplacement programs. Rather, each candidate's program is developed and delivered giving personal consideration to the uniqueness of the individual involved. Those individuals include hourly employees through corporate presidents/CEOs from more than 80 client companies.

WILLIAM M. LARRY
55 Meadowlark Lane
Williamsville, New York 14221
Residence: (716) 555-1813
Office: (716) 555-6232 Ex. 327

OBJECTIVE GENERAL MANAGEMENT - preferably with P&L responsibility - in a manufacturing organization committed to being a WORLD CLASS competitor.

SUMMARY Senior executive with progressive responsibilities in sales, marketing, operations, and general management for a technically sophisticated manufacturing organization. Grew company from start-up to worldwide market leadership. Committed to modern quality philosophies and tools; WCM, TQM, QFD, JIT, and SPC.

EXPERIENCE AND ACCOMPLISHMENTS

1980 to 1991 **HIGH-TECH BATTERIES, INC.**, division of Alternative Power, Ltd. Buffalo, NY
A manufacturer of high energy/high reliability backup batteries for military, aerospace, industrial, and commercial applications. Markets are worldwide.

General Manager, High-Tech Batteries, Inc. 1983 - 1991
Vice President, Alternative Power, Ltd. 1983 - 1991

Full profit and loss responsibility for directing growth of the division as a capable, high quality producer in an evolving marketplace. Manage new/improved processes, product development, operations, marketing, sales, and customer service. Spearhead the annual business planning/strategic planning processes. Lead the activities of 120 employees through five direct reports. Report to the President/CEO.

· Commercialized a high energy, high density, high voltage backup battery.

· Developed a worldwide distribution network; obtained Department of Commerce export licenses.

· Instilled a Total Quality Management philosophy in all employees incorporating WCM, SPC, and JIT principles. The following results accrued:
  - Rejections decreased 80%
  - Floor storage requirements reduced 65%
  - Reduced scrap by 62%
  - Increased productivity by 24 percentage points to 114%
  - Reduced inventory 50%
  - Reduced work-in-process inventory from 52% of schedule to 5%
  - Reduced throughput time from 10 days to 2-1/2 hours

· Licensed proprietary technology to companies in Korea and the Netherlands to increase worldwide demand and product availability.

· Established a relationship with a Japanese battery manufacturer for the resale of their products to enhance product line selection and distribution efficiency.

· Co-founded The Western Quality Network, a cooperative association of companies dedicated to sharing quality and business improvement knowhow.

· Presented "JIT...A Fast Track to Manufacturing Excellence" to a conference sponsored by the Association for Manufacturing Excellence.

Director of Sales and Marketing 1982 - 1983
North American Sales Manager 1980 - 1982

Originally responsible for North American sales of backup computer batteries. Scope grew to include sales and marketing responsibility for all APL product lines worldwide. Principle markets were Europe and Australia as well as North America. Managed three sales professionals plus support staff. Reported to the President.

· Analyzed product attributes, identified corresponding customer needs, and developed strategies targeting petroleum, aerospace, and oceanographic markets.

· Implemented the concept of "Selling in Depth"; built company-to-company relationships with R & D, engineering, and manufacturing in addition to purchasing.

1977 to 1980 **THE AMERICAN ABRASIVES COMPANY** Niagara Falls, NY
Electrominerals Division, Boron Products Department
Manufacturer and marketer of boron carbide materials for wear resistance, abrasive applications, and nuclear shielding.

Sales Engineer - Shielding Products

Developed and serviced the U.S. government and power generation markets for boron carbide nuclear shielding materials. Gained acceptance at architectural/engineering firms to specify company materials. Managed an advertising and literature program which established a visible presence in the market.

1974 to 1977 **NORTH AMERICAN CHEMICALS COMPANY** Wayne, NJ
A Fortune 200 chemical manufacturer with plants/sales offices worldwide.

Began as a laboratory scientist and progressed to regional sales/technical applications responsibilities for the paper, steel, mining, and water treating industries.

EDUCATION M.B.A., 1984, State University of New York at Buffalo, Buffalo, NY
B.S., Microbiology, 1974, California State University, Long Beach, CA

Continuing Education
Association for Manufacturing Excellence:"Activity Based Accounting," January, 1991, Costa Mesa, CA

Ernst and Young: "MRPII vs JIT," May, 1990, Buffalo, NY

Center for Quality and Productivity Improvement, University of Wisconsin: "Modern Quality and Productivity Improvement," May, 1988, Dallas, TX

Juran, J.M.: "Planning For Quality," February, 1988, San Francisco, CA

AFFILIATION Association for Manufacturing Excellence
American Society for Quality Control
National Electrical Manufacturers Association

PERSONAL Married, two children; US Army, 1966 - 1970, Captain; Excellent health; DOB:2-8-45

References and/or listing of presentations available upon request.

Power Resume Tip

If your resume is two pages long, add the word "continued" at the bottom of the first page, and put your name and the words "page 2" at the top of the second page just in case pages become separated once your resume is in the hands of your prospective employer.

A Techie Resume That Makes Sense

Don't Baffle Them With Jargon

"Individuals with a technical background might find it challenging to present their skills in a clear and concise manner," says Ann Wallace of Career Development Services.

While the inclusion of some jargon is good because it convinces the reviewer that you are intimate with the industry or specialty, you must remember that your resume might first be screened by nontechnical employees.

"In this resume Thomas Smith does an excellent job describing his background, accomplishments and expertise to potential employers," says Wallace. "More specifically, this combination format resume is attractive, free of irrelevant data and provides just enough information to provoke the reader's interest. Smith effectively presents his accomplishments through bulleted, short and punchy sentences."

The action words he has chosen, such as "developed," "directed" and "consulted" immediately emphasize his strengths.

"In addition, he sums up his technical qualifications succinctly for those interested in this sort of information. But, other than in the Technical Summary, Smith uses no other technical jargon."

Career Development Services

Career Development Services, located in Rochester, New York, is a nonprofit corporation providing comprehensive career planning services to individuals and organizations locally and nationally. The corporation is committed to identifying and addressing work force change issues through a variety of initiatives. These include assisting clients with formulating and implementing career and/or educational goals; consulting with employers to improve the quality of work life; and providing comprehensive resources, research and information on careers and related issues.

THOMAS A. SMITH

35 Main Street
Anytown, New York 54321
(123) 333-4444

Twenty years of progressive Management Information Systems experience in financial, human resources, sales/marketing, and manufacturing systems. Experienced manager with strengths in systems development and implementation for both large and small organizations.

SUMMARY OF QUALIFICATIONS

- Creatively resolved business systems issues.
- Organized and motivated project team members.
- Designed and implemented M.I.S. systems resulting in cost savings and improved departmental efficiencies.
- Successfully and consistently developed M.I.S. systems on-time and within budget.

TECHNICAL SUMMARY

- DOS/VSE
- CICS
- VSAM
- MSA/AR
- VM
- COBOL
- CMS
- PC-S
- CA/SORT
- CA/GL
- CA/AP
- CA/RAPS
- CA/DYNMT
- MSA/FIXED ASSETS

MANAGEMENT

- Managed the consolidation of financial and human resource systems of two major divisions.
- Developed, designed and implemented eighteen M.I.S. systems.
- Directed a staff of six programmers and systems analysts.
- Conducted feasibility and equipment analysis studies for corporate needs.
- Consulted in the installation of MSA and COMPUTER ASSOCIATES software packages.
- Developed new M.I.S. standards and procedures for the systems and operational areas.
- Planned and managed project implementation schedules.
- Managed a wide range of applications such as: payroll, sales, costing, budgeting, distribution, invoicing, accounts payable and receivables, order entry and inventory.

TRAINING

- Developed, implemented and conducted formal training programs and presentations for all levels of management.
- Conducted pre and post implementation training on installed packages.
- Conducted orientation and training sessions for new programming staff.
- Organized and presented professional seminars.

COMMUNICATIONS

- Interacted and coordinated with other corporate divisions and departments in the planning, development and implementation of new M.I.S. systems.
- Analyzed and selected various vendor packages.
- Developed written proposals to support new systems and programs.

EMPLOYERS

ABC Company	1988-present	Project Manager
XYZ Company	1980-1988	Senior Systems Analyst
XOX Products, Inc.	1978-1980	Operations Manager/Programmer

EDUCATION

Electronic Computer Programming Institute
Graduated with High Honors with
courses in RPG, COBOL and BAL, 1986

B.S., Business, 1978
Northern Georgia University

A.A.S., Business, 1976
Atlanta Community College

PERSONAL

- Past President and Director of the Anytown Lions Club
- Past President and Director of the ABC Management Club
- Past President of the Western Chapter of the Association of Systems Management
- Membership committee member of the Anytown Chapter of the Association of Systems Management

REFERENCES AVAILABLE UPON REQUEST

Power Resume Tip

Keep line length as short as possible. Studies have proven that it's easier to read information that's laid out in a longer block of copy with shorter lines than a short block of copy with long lines.

A 'Magic' Resume That's a Three-Time Winner

Built for the Toughest Competition

This resume and its subsequent updates have been so successful that its owner refers to it as the "Magic Resume." It has achieved its goal three times in a row: first, in attaining an in-house competitive promotion with a whopping 36 percent increase in salary, next in obtaining an even *more* lucrative position and, most recently, in securing comparable relocation employment in a constrained market—all this on the very first try!

The "magic" in this resume was conjured up by describing the job seeker's "experiences and accomplishments in an objective, succinct and interesting manner," says Jeannie Carlson. To do that, these eight rules that Carlson conveys to her clients were followed.

1. Eliminate the "I-me-my" focus by writing the resume in the first person implied. This facilitates a straightforward presentation without the impressions of egotism or false modesty.
2. Initiate sentences with action verbs. This moves along the otherwise mundane details and duties with sparkle.
3. Take inventory of specific accomplishments, identifying and itemizing them separately from the duties and responsibilities. This will show that you can do more for the prospective employer than the next person.
4. Be concise. Focus on developing an inverted pyramid of the last 10 years' experience, saying more about current employment.
5. Use terminology appropriate to your profession. Incorporate industry buzzwords. But be subtle so that you don't appear pretentious.
6. Use words that convey your personality to add individuality to an otherwise cookie-cutter document. For instance, an innovative personality might say that he "pioneered" rather than "developed."
7. Prioritize information within each job description to increase your chances that the reader will scan the most important items first.
8. Print the resume on good quality bond using bold and standard typefaces to highlight the resume and boost its overall appearance.

Jeannie Carlson

President, Viking Communications, Inc.

Jeannie Carlson is the Founder and Chief Executive Officer of Viking Communications, Inc., a professional writing company launched in 1987. Recognized in the Marquis edition of *Who's Who in America*, she has garnered numerous awards in fiction and nonfiction writing with multiple freelance credits in newspapers, periodicals and books nationwide. Her articles on resume preparation have appeared in such publications as the *St. Petersburg Times*, *Equal Opportunity Magazine* and *Veterans Chronicle*.

Note: The resume was printed as a fold-open 4-part brochure. The original cover page (which does not appear here) had the client's name, address, and phone number as well as an objective presented as an overview of expertise.

PROFILE Dedicated and meticulous health care professional with ten years proven record of accomplishments in personnel management, business functions and behavioral science. Proficient in planning, developing, supervising and implementing diversified policies, programs and procedures for optimum productivity and cost efficiency. Adept at both oral and written communication skills, interacting effectively with individuals from all walks of life. Excel at directing and motivating a cohesive staff in the successful attainment of corporate objectives.

EDUCATION

Master of Science in Counseling
TROY STATE UNIVERSITY, Dothan, Alabama
Completed: 10 Credit Hours Towards Degree Conferment

Bachelor of Arts in Psychology
RANDOLPH-MACON WOMAN'S COLLEGE, Lynchburg, Virginia
Degree Conferred: 1983

Department of Human Resources Training
STATE OF GEORGIA: 1977-1978 (98 Hours)
-CONFIDENTIALITY WORKSHOP
-ADULT WORKSHOPS & WORK ACTIVITIES I & I
-MINIMUM STANDARDS REVISIONS
-WORKSHOP ORGANIZATION
-NORMALIZATION WORKSHOP
-MANAGEMENT IN STATE GOVERNMENT, LEVEL I

Hypnoanalysis for Positive Sexual Functioning
SOCIETY OF MEDICAL HYPNOANALYSTS, Tampa, Florida
Certification Conferred: November 1982 (24 Hours)

Introduction to Neurolinguistic Programming (Mobile, Alabama)
Received One C.E. Credit: June 1982 (16 Hours)

How to Communicate Under Pressure; Dealing With Difficult People
ENTERPRISE STATE JUNIOR COLLEGE, Enterprise, Alabama
Received One C.E. Credit: April 1982 (16 Hours)

Instructors Course in Standard Emergency First Aid & Standard Emergency First Aid Course
AMERICAN RED CROSS, Savannah, Georgia
Certifications Conferred: June 1978 (8 Hours) & February 1978 (8 Hours)

Behavior Task Analysis Workshop
GEORGIA SOUTHERN COLLEGE, Statesboro, Georgia
Received One C.E. Credit: May 1978 (10 Hours)

CAREER HIGHLIGHTS

Business Office Manager: July 1992 - August 1993
CHARTER WOODS HOSPITAL
Dothan, Alabama

-Direct and manage the Business Office activities of a 75-bed Psychiatric Hospital, encompassing all day-to-day admissions, billing and collections functions, maximizing the hospital's financial position. Supervise the admissions, billing and collections staff, including hiring, orienting, training, monitoring, evaluating and counseling employees. Establish and maintain effective interdepartmental relationships with Needs Assessment, Utilization Review, Medical Records, and clinical services departments. Maintain multiple claims filed logs, review daily reports and accounts receivable documentation, oversee updating and posting, and make recommendations to the Controller for further account handling.

* Exceeded corporate accounts receivable management cash collection goal for all quarters, resulting in receiving Certificates of Achievement for Outstanding Accounts Receivable Management.
* Achieved status in the Top 10 Hospitals with the lowest Accounts Receivable days for the past 2 quarters.

Business Office Manager: May 1988 - July 1992
HUMANA HOSPITAL - ENTERPRISE
Enterprise, Alabama

-Managed a staff of 25 personnel in the daily Business Office operations of a 135-bed Medical-Surgical Hospital. Supervised and coordinated all activities involving the Admissions, Billing, Collections, Switchboard and Front Cashier departments. Accountable for all Accounts Receivable, Billing and Collections outcome. Utilized the MED A system for Medicare billings. Dealt with bankruptcy litigation, analyzed and authorized legal suits, and represented the company in contested legal suits.

* Reduced bad debt in the first 2 months to below corporate goal.
* Introduced and implemented cross-training of department personnel.
* Created and implemented an effective reorganization plan for the Business Office to facilitate work flow in accordance with employee cutbacks.
* Developed New Task Oriented Employee Job Descriptions.
* Promoted from Insurance Billing Clerk to Admission Supervisor (7/89) to Business Office Manager (12/91).

Behavior Education Instructor: February 1986-August 1987
NUTRI/SYSTEM WEIGHT LOSS CENTER
Dothan, Alabama

-Scheduled and presented all weight loss classes and performed client evaluations of eating behaviors. Taught classes in Positive Self Thought and Image, Thought Focusing, Relaxation, Exercise, Nutrition, Assertiveness, and Motivation. Took blood pressures, weighed clients, measured and supervised client compliance with food program. Performed inventory control, fee collection, assembly and charging of client orders, and booking consultation appointments.

* Served as Office Manager in her absence.
* Compiled monthly newsletter.
* Traveled to other locations to service clients in more remote areas.

(OVER)

CONTINUED **Registrar/Instructor/Owner**: May 1982-May 1986
ENTERPRISE LAMAZE CHILDBIRTH EDUCATION CENTER
Enterprise, Alabama
-Responsible for operations management of Lamaze Childbirth Education Program. Performed records management, including accounts payable and accounts receivable. Promoted the business via advertising flyers, newspaper and television announcements. Acted as Instructor, selecting appropriate visual and auditory aids, presenting material, arranging guest speakers, coordinating and conducting hospital labor and delivery room tours, and providing individual instruction to couples. As Registrar, provided course information, collected fees, and assigned instructors to couples.
* Promoted from Registrar to Instructor, May 1983.
* Purchased business from owner, June 1983.

Assistant/Office Manager: September 1981-September 1985
ENTERPRISE MEDICAL CLINIC
Enterprise, Alabama
-Assisted and managed the Behavioral Medicine Office of a Physician and Licensed Professional Counselor. Scheduled appointments, screened patients, set up patient accounts, collected payments, and handled inventory. Maintained and organized files, video and cassette tape libraries and patient handouts. Submitted and expedited patient insurance form documentation. Supervised one employee, trained new employees, handled scheduling, and coordinated work flow.
* Substituted for the Pediatric Nurse in her absence.
* Created patient handouts.

Instructor Supervisor (Instructor II): September 1977-September 1978
STATE OF GEORGIA MERIT SYSTEM, DEPT. OF HUMAN RESOURCES
Riceboro, Georgia
-Supervised 7 instructors and instructor aids of retarded and handicapped children and adults. Assured the proper maintenance of student records as well as the quality and suitability of the curriculum. Conducted in-service training to staff as required by the state of Georgia. Monitored and coordinated time worked, comp time and substitute instructors. Assumed the responsibilities of Center Bus Driver as needed. Obtained work contracts, performed time studies, arranged for and accompanied clients on health service trips, and traveled throughout Georgia for workshops and meetings.
* Advanced from Instructor to Instructor Supervisor after 9 months.
* Designed new adult workshops and activities.
* Organized and directed the local Special Olympics between counties for approximately 100 participants.

PUBLIC SPEAKING
Cradle Club, HUMANA HOSPITAL, Enterprise, Alabama: 1988
Weight Loss Instructor, NUTRI/SYSTEM: 1986-1987
Special Olympics, Hinesville, Georgia: 1978
Minimum Standards, DEPARTMENT OF HUMAN RESOURCES: 1977-1978
Lamaze Instructor, PREPARED CHILDBIRTH: 1982-1986
Sunday School: 1982-1983

Wearing the Old School Ties

Putting Your Best Foot Forward

A recent *New Yorker* cartoon depicts a gravestone on which is inscribed something like: "John B. Rutherford. Princeton, 1926-1930."

Indeed some of us do place too much importance on *where* someone went to school, but it's easy to see why this candidate would list his degrees and the institutions at which he attained them right at the top. He immediately positions himself as a scientist with a terrific aptitude for management.

What's more, the resume, by being concise and packed with a great deal of information in just one page, demonstrates that the candidate probably is someone "respected for ability to communicate" as stated in the Personal Qualifications section, points out John Dugan, President of JH Dugan & Associates.

"This resume is concise, historical and thorough without being verbose, to the point, informative and convincing," says Dugan.

Note that the candidate used a smaller typeface to pack a great deal of information onto one side of a page.

While this might have some drawbacks, "it saves readers time and insures that all of this candidate's impressive credentials are read at almost a single glance," says Dugan.

John Dugan
President, JH Dugan & Associates

JH Dugan & Associates is an executive search firm specializing in the plastics industry and is located in Carmel, California. Its President, John Dugan, is past chairman of the National Association of Executive Recruiters and has been director for 10 years.

MBA, Harvard Business School
BS, Chemical Engineering, MIT

objective

Industrial Marketing/Sales or General Management.

background summary

General Manager with experience in product management, market research, OEM and distributor sales, and manufacturing.

personal qualifications

Known as a quick learner with strong analytical and interpersonal skills. Respected for ability to communicate with all levels involved in delivering an industrial product to market—from design and production to the customer's management, engineering, and purchasing staff.

business experience

1984-1985 — **INDUSTRY, INC.** — **CITY, STATE**

Privately owned contractor of hazardous chemical waste cleanup services in the Northeast. Sales of $2.5 million, with 36 employees at two sites.

General Manager. P&L responsibility with authority for all non-accounting aspects of the business including direction of the New Jersey branch office. Management responsibility for oil spill cleanup contracts in the Caribbean Basin and the Port of New York & New Jersey, serving two oil company cooperatives.

- Reduced losses by $1.0 million from 1983 levels.
- Reduced employee turnover through improved consistency and fairness in personnel practices.
- Reduced and hired New Jersey branch manager and operations supervisor, and salesmen for both operations. Succeeded in attracting highly qualified individuals in spite of extremely limited budget.
- Negotiated all company cleanup contracts, including a major subcontract for the EPA.
- Changed suppliers for major product line, resulting in margin increase from 25% to 45%.
- Prepared 1985 annual plan and budget—a first for the business.

1981-1984 — **CORPORATION** — **CITY, STATE**

Privately held manufacturer of automotive interior parts, with annual sales of over $50 million.

Product/Account Manager. Market development responsibility for non-automotive, and direct sales responsibility for Chrysler and American Motors accounts, representing $1.5 million in sales and $400 thousand in tooling.

- Established product line strategy, including pricing, distribution, packaging and promotion for the company's first non-automotive product.
- Negotiated numerous price increases due to engineering changes, totaling approximately 100% by six months into production.
- Prepared and presented technical reviews for customer engineering staff; succeeded in getting product specifications revised to meet actual production capabilities.
- Planned and directed company booth at industry trade shows.

1976-1979 — **COMPANY** — **CITY, STATE**

Process Engineer. Responsible for process improvement, design and controls. Estimated product costs and production standards. Coordinated production of test products for marketing and product development.

education

(date) — **HARVARD GRADUATE SCHOOL OF BUSINESS ADMINISTRATION** — **BOSTON, MASSACHUSETTS**

Master in Business Administration, June 1981. General management curriculum with emphasis on marketing and operations. Summer job in 1980 as a marketing consultant to an aftermarket automotive parts manufacturer.

(date) — **MASSACHUSETTS INSTITUTE OF TECHNOLOGY** — **CAMBRIDGE, MASSACHUSETTS**

Bachelor of Science in Chemical Engineering, June 1976, Varsity skiing, four years; co-captain senior year.

A Resume That Grabs and Keeps On Grabbing

Clear Layout Focuses on Accomplishments

The generous amounts of white space and the boldface type grabbed Claudia A. Gentner, cofounder and senior vice president of Seagate Associates, when she first looked at it.

"I immediately understood that this candidate was a planning executive at the vice president level," said the career consultant. "All of that happened in a moment."

"In the next instant," she continued, "the reader can *absorb* the writer's experience in three management chunks, giving the impression of stability and commitment to organization. "If the reader still has interest, in the next moment, company names become evident."

Then the reader gets to the "real content" of the resume—the accomplishment statements.

Gentner praises the elegance of this resume. For instance, she points to the summary at the top. "My preference is for a brief summary statement that doubles as an objective. Note the use of the term Planning Executive. What does this person do? Succinctly: 'Formulate business objectives and develop plans to achieve them.' That's elegantly stated. Just enough words to explain the focus of the candidate's job function."

Gentner also states that those who know this candidate or who read his resume closely "recognize he's a transportation planning executive. But his planning skills are certainly transferable to other contexts and his intention here is to appeal to a broader readership than the transportation industry."

Claudia A. Gentner
Senior Vice President, Seagate Associates, Inc.

In addition to her responsibilities with the New Jersey-based career transition consulting firm, Gentner is also a director of Outplacement International, a privately held corporation owned by regionally prominent career transition consulting firms. Gentner established Seagate's Business Information Center, which is the first such facility in the outplacement industry dedicated to the information needs of job seekers. She is a frequent contributor to leading human resources publications and is listed in *Who's Who in Finance and Industry*.

PLANNING EXECUTIVE

Formulate business objectives and develop plans to achieve them.

1983-present **Vice President, Resource Planning**
Purolator Courier Corp., Basking Ridge, N.J.

Through a staff of 60, direct all planning activities for the U.S. Courier Division's transportation network, facilities, equipment, purchasing and procurement.

- Creating the company's first formal tactical and strategic operations-oriented planning group.
- Developed and managed the capital budget for expenditures averaging $57+ million/year.
- Selected Indianapolis as the firm's air service hub. Negotiated the site development contracts and directed the facilities construction program.
- Developed aircraft fleet plans and schedules. Directed the acquisition of a fleet of large turbo-prop and heavy jet aircraft. Negotiated long-term aircraft operating agreements with independent contractors.
- Designed and implemented a plan to eliminate excess motor vehicle capacity through a sale and the leaseback of fewer, more fuel-efficient vehicles. Annual cost savings of $6.1 million.

1978-83 **Vice President**
Simat, Helliesen and Eichner, Inc., New York, N.Y.

Senior project director for a firm of transportation industry economists and planners who provide consulting services to companies involved in transportation.

- Created complete business, organizational, operational and financial plans for air and ground carriers.
- Directed strategic and tactical planning projects involving market and marketing studies, cost and pricing models, forecasting, route and fleet planning, flight equipment and capital investment evaluations.
- Prepared diversification studies and economic analyses of potential mergers.
- Developed strategies, evidence and testimony in antitrust litigations and labor arbitration proceedings.

1965-1978 **Senior Director, Passenger Pricing**
Director, Freight Pricing
American Airlines, Inc., New York, N.Y.

Formulated and implemented profitable and innovative passenger, freight, mail and express pricing policies with supporting regulatory, marketing and operational strategies.

- **Instituted several cost-related system passenger fare changes, including the precedent-setting "Super Saver" program, that increased annual revenues $103+ million.**
- **Created the company's strategic position, with all economic supporting evidence, for the CAB's investigation of all U.S. carriers' pricing policies and rate levels.**
- **Served as the company's representative on passenger and cargo-related matters to the International Air Transportation Association and the Air Transportation Association of America.**

EDUCATION

BA Political Science, 1963
Providence College

Graduate work in Law and Business (36 credits), 1963-1965
St. John's University Law School

Power Resume Tip

Pepper your resume with results-oriented accomplishments that spell B-E-N-E-F-I-T-S to employers. If your resume reads like a job description, you've got work to do.

A Place for Bells and Whistles

When Repetition Bears Repeating

"Formatting, writing and layout should always be subordinate to strategy in developing an effective resume," says Mark Gisleson, a resume writer with more than 10,000 resumes and cover letters to his credit.

While he follows traditional resume formats, Gisleson says he also uses "cheap tricks, bells and whistles, inspired writing—and whatever works" to manipulate the reader—pulling him or her into the copy and creating a need to meet the person whose name is at the top of the page.

Gisleson is quick to point out that he uses key information over and over again in the sample resume. "In this case, the client's job experience was unrelated to her objective. It was important to promote her related skills since her intended audience was an anonymous government bureaucrat.

"Because government standard forms for hiring (SF 171s) are designed to be repetitious and exhaustive, I have found that you often need to hit federal bureaucrats over the head several times before you can get your point across."

He adds, "In this case, we began by listing skills appropriate to the position. In effect, we defined the job before ever mentioning the position of 'project manager.' A Related Experience section was then created to highlight her internship, which was directly related to the position. This job description gives examples of the skills mentioned in the summary, providing reinforcement.

"The final repetition comes in the Continuing Education section where the client's VA experience is trotted out again, this time in the form of on-the-job training."

Gisleson considers the artful use of repetition one of his most effective strategies.

As a final touch, Gisleson likes to use an Interests or Activities section to demonstrate client "physical fitness or concern about health, intellectual activity not related to work and just about anything that is a little different or unusual."

Mark Gisleson
Writer

Doing business as Gisleson Writing Services, Mark Gisleson has worked with more than 4,000 job seekers nationwide since 1987, writing resumes, letters, SF 171s and personal statements for applicants to graduate schools. A former manager for Professional Resume & Writing Service and CareerPro, Gisleson's advice column, *JQ&A: Answers to Questions About Jobs*, is syndicated through City Media News & Information.

KIMBERLY BROWN

1558 Albany, St. Paul, MN 55108
612 644-6408

SUMMARY *of* PROFESSIONAL QUALIFICATIONS

- Highly dedicated new graduate with well-developed communication and organizational skills; strong project management experience.
- Goal-oriented; able to make effective use of all available resources.
- Self-starter; works well independently or as member of a team.

EDUCATION

COLLEGE OF ST. JOSEPH, St. Benedict, MN
Bachelor of Arts Degree, May 1994
Liberal Studies major.
Advanced coursework taken in SCIENCE and MANAGEMENT:
- Microbiology · Chemistry · Anatomy
- Management · Marketing · Business

RELATED EXPERIENCE

VETERAN'S ADMINISTRATION HOSPITAL, St. Benedict, MN
Administrative Internship, February 1994 to May 1994

Reported to the Staff Assistant for Clinical Affairs.

Independently researched and designed a Total Quality Improvement directory which was approved and implemented by the hospital. This same directory was subsequently adapted for official use by the Nursing Program at St. Joseph's.

At the request of the Hospital Director, reviewed and analyzed the hospital's committee system, focusing on issues related to member participation, ability to implement change, and committee's status (regulation mandated, etc.).

EMPLOYMENT

CARSON PIRIE SCOTT, St. Benedict, MN
Sales Associate – SHOE DEPARTMENT, 1994 to Present

Provide immediate and attentive customer service, assisting with selections of moderate to better shoes and accessories.

Additional responsibilities include stocking, inventory, balancing cash registers and answering customer questions.

MONTGOMERY WARD, St. Benedict, MN
Sales Associate, 1990 to 1994

Worked with all facets of store sales from customer service to returns, as well as assisting with display set-ups and promotions.

Trained and supervised new personnel; functioned as assistant manager as necessary.

MIDWESTERN MECHANICAL, Blaine, MN
Janitor, 1989 to 1990

CONTINUING EDUCATION

VETERAN'S ADMINISTRATION: Ongoing training in VA administrative, staffing and committee structures, lines of communication and authority.

CARSON PIRIE SCOTT/MONTGOMERY WARD: On-the-job sales, merchandising, and customer service training.

COMMUNITY

Active participant in VISTO, a St. Joseph's sponsored service organization.
Assisted with a latchkey program at Kennedy Elementary, working with children in grades 1-5.

INTERESTS

- Vice President, St. John's/St. Joseph's Karate Club.
- Swimming, skiing and horseback riding.

The Ten-Second Resume

How to Make It Out of the Slush Pile

"Statistically," says Laurie Hadley, placement director at Valley Training Centers in West Virginia, "an employer spends approximately 10 seconds on a resume before it is tossed into the 'no' pile. By using bulleted statements and taking advantage of fonts and layouts, you can keep your resume out of that pile—and *make an impression strong enough in those critical 10 seconds to get yourself an interview*.

"The most common resume mistakes are made," she adds, "because resume writers do not realize two important facts: One, resumes lead to interviews and, two, interviews lead to job offers."

She adds, "Don't try to secure a job offer with a resume. Forget detailed job descriptions, addresses, references and such when writing a resume. Make your qualifications and accomplishments stand out. *Save the rest for the interview*."

Laurie Sykes Hadley
Placement Director, Valley Training Centers, Inc.

Valley Training Centers (VTC), Inc., located in Martinsburg, WV, is a computer and business school that offers training to adult students and businesses. VTC is committed to the development of graduates who are proficient in occupational readiness, employability skills and technical excellence. In addition to her work at VTC, Hadley is a resume writer. Through a contract with the Department of Veterans' Affairs, she prepares resumes for veterans. In addition, she produces advertising layouts and business forms for businesses and individuals.

Administrative Assistant
with 6 years experience
seeks new challenge

Cathy L. Gusciora

1500 David Stafford Drive
Martinsburg, WV 25401
(304) 555-0979

Skill Summary

- **Six years experience as an administrative assistant utilizing the following skills:**

Computer:
MS DOS
Windows
ACC PAC
Lotus 1-2-3
dBase III Plus
WordPerfect 5.1
WordPerfect 6.0

General Office:
SuperWrite
Transcription
Collections
Type 90+ wpm
Telephone Etiquette
Editing/Proofreading
Payroll (including taxes)

Administrative:
Budget Analysis
Employee Training
Office Management
Quarterly & Annual Reports
Sales Manual Layout & Design
Advertising Campaign Designs
Corporate Office/Staff Liaison

Employment Experience

Administrative Assistant - Sales Division, George Cooke Computers, Martinsburg, WV
1988 - Present

- Provided administrative support to sales division with annual sales of $2.5 Million
- Maintained personnel files and processed payroll (including commissions and bonuses) for 25 sales specialists
- Worked closely with corporate vice president to prepare reports, sales plans, and budget analysis for staff and board meetings
- Compiled information and computer designed sales manuals and advertising campaigns
- Acted as liaison between corporate office and staff
- Responsible for training clerical support staff
- **Corporate Employee of the Year - 1993**

Receptionist/ Secretary, Davis Lewis & Unger, Attorneys at Law, Martinsburg, WV - 1986-88

- Acted as initial contact person for all clientele at busy criminal defense firm
- Provided clerical support to office administrator
- Responsible for developing and teaching seminar for office employees on telephone reception
- Represented firm in various civic activities

Education

Office Technology Certificate - Secretarial Specialty, Valley Training Centers, Martinsburg, WV - 1988

A Record That Speaks for Itself

A Resume Approach That's Definitely Not for Everyone

"This resume is the most unusual, yet effective, that ever crossed my desk," says Robert Half, founder of Robert Half International Inc., one of the world's largest personnel recruiting firms. "It has only 36 words. However, it landed the candidate eight interviews from which he got four job offers in a short period of time."

You can hardly argue with such success!

"Since the candidate was applying for a position as an accountant," notes Half, "those companies that viewed the resume were fully familiar with the quality of his experience and education. In addition, the resume clearly points out his achievement—the most important feature of any resume."

This candidate graduated from top schools with high grades and earned a senior accountant position within three years. This, indeed, is a record that, as Half says, "speaks for itself."

Half also points out that this resume contains "no reference to goals, but in my opinion such statements are generally not necessary on a resume and often tend to eliminate qualified candidates who include goals that might be too limited."

The advantages of this very short and sweet approach? "Well," says Half, "it will be read in its entirety by almost everyone. It contains all the essential facts. It establishes the candidate's successes. And it's professional, yet novel."

Robert Half
Founder, Robert Half International Inc.

Although he founded one of the most renowned personnel recruiting firms more than 40 years ago, Robert Half is still an active voice in the area of careers and job search. His latest book is *Finding, Hiring, and Keeping The Best Employees*, now in paperback from John Wiley & Sons, Inc. Robert Half International Inc. specializes in accounting and financial professionals through its Robert Half division and Accountemps, its temporary placement service. The company has more than 175 offices and is listed on the New York Stock Exchange.

Charles Smith, CPA
123 Monadnock Road
Newton, MA 02167

Harvard BA 1986 *
Harvard MBA 1988 *
* Graduated top 15%

1988 to 1991—Brown, Gray & Co., Big Six CPA firm.
Achieved Senior Accountant status in three years.

Spare the Details...Please

Resume Advice for Older Job Applicants

When 64-year-old John Smith met Peggy Hendershot, his resume was three pages long and crammed with highly detailed, technical information. As you can see, Hendershot, director of Career Planning Services at Career Vision, helped Smith fashion a highly readable two-page document.

"The resume is not an autobiography, but a teaser to encourage a personal contact and interview," says Hendershot. "In most cases, the job seeker is unable to tailor each resume for specific positions. Therefore, the identification of transferable skills becomes critical. In many cases, similar skills are used in various positions. It is helpful to stress different abilities, rather than emphasize similar activities repeatedly."

Smith's resume demonstrates technical and supervisory skills, individual and group problem-solving capabilities and leadership skill in an electronic research and development environment. And it does this while providing the reader plenty of "breathing room" with white space, lines between bulleted items and a wide left margin.

"Smith's resume is a flexible tool for his job search effort," says Hendershot. "In the Professional Summary, the job seeker has identified the type of responsibilities for which he is best suited and supports that with specific statements in the body of the resume that also demonstrate the strengths Smith claimed to have."

Peggy Hendershot
Director of Career Planning Services, Career Vision

Peggy Hendershot is the director of career planning services for Career Vision. The firm, which has offices in the Chicago area, offers a distinctive approach to career planning for individuals and organizations. Counselors help individuals with an improved self-understanding through a comprehensive assessment process that integrates aptitude, interests, personality, values and skills. This multiple assessment is invaluable in the identification of appropriate career paths and/or the selection of continuing education programs.

JOHN SMITH
9876 Main Street
Small Town, IL 35455

PROFESSIONAL SUMMARY

Electronics Engineer with over twenty years of experience in research and development. Background in telecommunications, fire alarms, and consumer electronics. Skilled at problem identification and resolution. Seven patents.

WORK EXPERIENCE

Major Corporation, International **1979-1989**
Serious, Illinois
Technical Team Leader

- Engineering/Production liaison for Digital Loop Carrier, "DLC". Successfully identified and solved design related production problems.
- Wrote requirements documents and test plans for Digital Loop Carrier ($24 million system).
- Led hardware design of an Automated Test System which resulted in a 50% saving of test time.
- Simplified test procedures, cutting three hours from the final test of each DLC system.

Engineering Supervisor

- Supervised design of Channel Bank, both for voice and data. Accounted for $2 million annual sales.
- Coordinated the design of T-carrier synchronization system, from start to production. $1 million annual sales.
- Initiated corrective action on the ASIC Custom Integrated Circuit and switch-mode power supply, saving $200,000.
- Led the complete design of division's first microprocessor controlled system and first U.L. listing.

ABC Electronics, Inc. **1977-1979**
Aurora, Illinois
Manufacturer of First Alert home smoke detector and industrial fire alarm systems.

- Engineering group leader for industrial fire alarm systems.
- Developed and guided a product through Underwriters Laboratories, and three similar approval agencies in Canada, Germany, and Denmark. Visited the European agencies.

XYZ Electronics **1962-1977**
Chicago, Illinois
Design and manufacture of television receivers for Sears Roebuck

- Managed a TV engineering department with 20 engineers and technical staff
- Directed engineering of first solid state color television receiver from prototype through production.
- Reduced cost of production of color TV receivers, saving $200,000 in one year.
- Extensive research and development role included: UHF varactor tuner, sound, chroma, C.R.T. circuits, scan, high voltage, video, transistorization, computer simulation.

EDUCATION

Illinois Institute of Technology
- MBA, (Elected Sigma Iota Epsilon)

Illinois Institute of Technology
- MSEE (Elected Sigma XI)
- BSEE

Midwest College of Engineering
- 1980 post-graduate microprocessor design course
- Recent in-house courses: digital signal processor, effective communication, "Novations", career planning and counseling.

PROFESSIONAL ACTIVITIES

- Registered Professional Engineer of State of Illinois
- Senior Member I.E.E.E.
- Past Chairman I.E.E.E. Consumer Electronics Society
- Former member I.E.E.E. T.V. Measurements Standards Committee

REFERENCES WILL BE FURNISHED UPON REQUEST.

Power Resume Tip

When detailing current positions, use the present tense. When describing previous experiences, use past tense. Also, use short phrases, and leave out unnecessary articles, such as "I," "the," "an," etc.

A Zero-Based Resume That Works

Sticking to the Basics

"Realizing that a potential employer is buying capabilities," says Joseph W. Hollis of Bernard Haldane Associates in Oklahoma City, "John Smith designed his resume to show his past achievements, thus emphasizing his capabilities."

Smith has kept his resume to one page and provides it in a very readable style. By using boldface type, he is able to draw attention to his skills and abilities with just a cursory glance from a resume-weary recruiter, human resources employee or possible future boss.

"Most executives are interested in what you have accomplished in past positions," adds Hollis, "so this type of functional, or zero-based, resume is very effective at highlighting what you are capable of achieving for them."

The resume is a tool to help you get in front of a potential employer, reminds Hollis. It will not get you a job, but it can set the stage for your interview.

"Know your resume inside and out," he says. "Be able to expand on all of your achievements. Remember: Your resume is the only thing a potential employer has to judge your capabilities; thus, look at the resume as your interview outline and script."

Finally, Hollis says, this type of resume will allow you to tailor it to the targeted executive, position and/or company by simply changing your objective and realigning your list of achievements. For example, Smith could change his resume by replacing "operations" in his objective with "production," "labor relations," "material handling" and so forth.

Joseph W. Hollis
Bernard Haldane Associates

For the past three years, Joseph Hollis has served as a career adviser with Bernard Haldane Associates in Oklahoma City, using his 25 years of business experience to assist clients in developing and executing effective marketing strategies for their job searches.

JOHN B. SMITH
1234 Second Ave
Oklahoma City, OK 73120
(405) 555-1212

OBJECTIVE:

To assist the operations area of an organization in achieving its potential by using my developing, organizing, communicating and implementing experience interacting with all levels of management.

QUALIFICATIONS:

More than 20 years experience in the public and private sectors which includes: team development; operations management; personnel management; policy formulation and implementation; improving performance and providing quality customer support. Directed the administrations and operations of a firm with a $10 million annual operating budget.

ACHIEVEMENTS

INCREASED PRODUCTION 300%
Organized and **developed** a senior level management team credited with a **300%** increase in maintenance shop quality, a **15%** reduction in customer complaints, a **53%** reduction in unemployment costs and the development of a new job costing program.

INCREASED PRODUCTION 41%
Redesigned the production flow, **developed** a more efficient production process and **achieved** a **41%** increase in production. **Formed** a team of supervisors and line employees to participate in production study.

INCREASED PRODUCTION 40%
Coordinated the efforts of the materials, assembly, and fabrication departments to develop an efficient production process. **Planned** the production and **coordinated** the process of each department so that the subassemblies would be available timely. **Achieved** a **40%** increase in production.

DECREASED INVENTORY BY 34%
Analyzed inventory to define excess or obsolete stock. **Negotiated** return or sale of overstock. **Implemented** the use of planned reorder and stock quantities to maintain desired inventory levels which resulted in a **34%** decrease in inventory.

FIRST MULTI-YEAR LABOR AGREEMENT IN 10 YEARS
Eliminated employee/union issues by involving employees in policy making. **Directed** employee teams in the analysis of company policies including safety policy, accident policy, customer services policy, etc. Leading to the first successfully **negotiated** multi-year labor agreement in 10 years.

EXPERIENCE:

Director of Operations
American Home Delivery

Assistant Administrator
Director Administration
Central Texas Transportation
and Parking Authority

General Manager, Operations
Compusamp, Inc.

Materials Manager
Geolograph Pioneer, Inc.

EDUCATION:

B.B.A. Management — University of Texas

Use Action Verbs, Not Marshmallow Words

Convince Them of Your Accomplishments

Here's a resume that can almost leave a reader out of breath! It's brimming with action words that go a long way toward convincing a recruiter that this candidate has done something with his work life.

"Action words such as 'directed,' 'developed' and 'implemented' show direct involvement in what the organization does," says Richard H. Jackson. He's president of Considine, Jackson & Associates, Inc., an outplacement firm based in Lexington, Kentucky. "Marshmallow verbs such as 'coordinated,' on the other hand, leave one wondering what exactly you accomplished."

On Nicholas Clark's resume, we find lots of action words. What's more, we find lots of numbers. Jackson notes that candidates can "make the statement of accomplishments have impact by using percentages or qualifying numerical statistics—dollars saved, costs reduced, etc. Avoid rounded-off figures," he notes, since "nobody hits it exactly on the nose. Use 9 percent or 12 percent, rather than 10 percent and 15 percent."

Notice also that this resume completely shuns extraneous details. Jackson advises candidates to avoid personal information such as hobbies, religious affiliations and marital status, but to include civic organizations, especially if you are an officer. However, do not make it a long list, he says. "When would you have had time for work?"

Richard H. Jackson
President, Considine, Jackson & Associates, Inc.

Considine, Jackson & Associates, part of the Right Associates International Network, is a corporate outplacement firm located in Lexington, Kentucky, and is a member of the Association of Outplacement Consulting Firms. CJ&A works with individuals who have been involuntarily released from their organizations; encompassing a broad range of candidates from clerical, middle managers, professionals up to and including lawyers, doctors and Ph.D.s. The development of a resume is one of the first steps before the firm helps the client establish a comprehensive marketing program.

Nicholas H. Clark
273 Edgewater Drive
Lexington, Kentucky 40502

(606) 555-0027

OBJECTIVE: Managerial opportunity in Quality Assurance

QUALIFICATIONS: Experienced Director of Quality Assurance with progressive and broad range of management and technical skills in quality system development and implementation. B.S. Degree in Chemistry, graduated cum laude.

PROFESSIONAL HISTORY:

April 1986 - PRESENT

XYZ Company
Lexington, Kentucky
Divisional Sales: $500 million

July 1989 - Present

Divisional Director of Quality Assurance

Responsibilities: Budgeting, centralizing, managing, and developing multi-plant Quality Assurance Program. Four direct reports, supervising combined staff of 50.

Significant Accomplishments:

. **Developed strategic plan and began implementation of Total Quality System resulting in significant productivity improvements.**

. **Incorporated ISO-9000 series quality standard requirements and Malcolm Baldridge National Quality Award Criteria into Total Quality System.**

. **Created vendor and internal quality certification programs.**

. **Established quality training plans including statistical, problem-solving and teambuilding techniques for continuous improvement.**

. **Design and published quality manual, and developed and conducted quality system audit program.**

April 1986 - July 1989

Director of Quality Assurance and Process Control

Responsibilities: Established and implemented the quality policy and direction for division. Technical/Marketing representative for customers and professional organizations.

Significant Accomplishments:

. **Designed and implemented strategic plan for quality improvement resulting in increased market share and winning the XYZ Company and Westinghouse Quality Award.**

. **Created quality training plan to include statistical techniques and quality concepts and provided instructional support.**

. **Developed and implemented quality management system to meet international, military, and regulatory standards.**

. **Planned company's Worldwide Quality Conference in 1987, 1988, and 1989.**

September 1983 - April 1986

ABC Company
Lexington, Kentucky
Annual Sales: $135 million

Corporate Quality Assurance Engineer

Responsibilities: Statistical process control program, vendor qualification, and quality training.

Significant Accomplishments:

- Designed and implemented comprehensive statistical process control program to meet military and automotive specifications.
- Established vendor qualification process and conducted vendor audits.
- Developed and implemented formal problem analysis and corrective action process.
- Initiated and performed ongoing plantwide meetings on quality and manufacturing topics/issues; e.g., SPC, clean rooms, etc.

March 1981 - September 1983

EFG Company
Lexington, Kentucky
Annual Sales: $100 million

Quality Control Manager

Responsibilities: Management of personnel and supplies for the Chemistry and In-Process Laboratories, as well as government and customer inspectors.

Significant Accomplishments:

- Enhanced and maintained comprehensive quality system to meet MIL-Q-9858A specification requirements.
- Conducted vendor audits and customer order reviews to assure compliance to specification requirements.
- Developed and began implementation of statistical techniques for process optimization.

January 1973 - February 1977

United States Navy
Vietnam Veteran - Hospital Corpsman

EDUCATION:

Bachelor of Science, Chemistry - 1981 (Cum Laude)
Penn State University

Additional professional courses:
- Statistical techniques and design of experiments from the American Supplier Institute, Hewlett-Packard, Motorola, and Shainin
- Quality systems and auditing from Spindler Associates, Philip Crosby Associates, Motorola, and Institute of Quality Assurance
- Executive, financial, marketing, and manufacturing training from Goldratt, Wharton, and Kellogg.

PROFESSIONAL ASSOCIATIONS:

American Society for Quality Control
American Chemical Society

Power Resume Tip

Show your resume to friends, family members or trusted co-workers, preferably those who are familiar with your skills. They may be able to remind you of accomplishments or skills you have overlooked, or help with organization and content problems.

Make It Easy On the Reader

Getting Rid of Overemphasis

The format that David Robertson uses in his resume has worked effectively for people seeking positions in everything from customer services to mid-level management, according to John Jungclaus, owner of CareerPro Services in Harrisburg, Lancaster and York, Pennsylvania.

"Through the use of specific 'eye-catchers,' " he says, "this resume entices the individual reviewing resumes to read it before all others."

Enhancements include increasing the size of the name of the person submitting the resume, dividing the general structure into specific areas providing small segments of relevant information to read and beginning with a synopsis of the person's background.

Emphasis using bullets, font changes and boldfaced words are kept to a minimum to avoid burdening the reader with overemphasis.

Robertson starts off each of his positions with a brief overview of his work experience, then provides pertinent information on his skills, knowledge, responsibilities and experiences. Bulleted items are concise, easy to read and of real worth to the reader.

"Remember," says Jungclaus, "an employer wants to know what benefit you will become to the organization. In other words, how much can you save them and how much can you make them."

John Jungclaus
CareerPro Services

John Jungclaus, the owner of CareerPro Services, is a former regional director for a mid-Atlantic career development and resume service. As regional director, he managed 23 offices throughout northern Virginia, Washington, D.C., Maryland and Pennsylvania. Jungclaus has conducted numerous seminars and workshops in resume development and transition assistance and has developed resume packages for individuals in career transitions. He is a member of the Professional Association of Resume Writers.

DAVID R. ROBERTSON
750 East Park Drive
Harrisburg, Pennsylvania 17111
(717) 555-8388

Professional Synopsis

Over 4 years diversified experience in mechanical engineering providing design, development, and modification of hand and pneumatic actuated tools used in the termination of electrical connectors. The ideal position will provide for a wide range of experience in the engineering field particularly in design and project management.

Professional Experience

March 1990 to Present

Harris Products, Inc. - Harrisburg, Pennsylvania
Have held the following positions at Harris Products, Inc.

Product Engineer I and II **(May 1992 to Present)**

▸ Manage the modifications, retooling and new design of four hand-tool lines: Modular Crimp, Dual Action, Shock Absorbent Head and Reciprocal Action tools. Provide extensive tool reviews and analyses to meet the demands of the customer. Conduct studies and work various projects to determine cost-effective measures in correcting production line problems. Identify, select, and recommend capital equipment to improve production quality and output.

- Resolve customer inquires at all levels from general tool operation to design specifications and specialized modifications. Clients include corporations in Japan, Singapore, England, and Germany.
- Effectively managed six projects totaling $845,000 to 10 percent below budgets.
- Provided consulting assistance in development of various connector tooling and plastic mold designs.

Machine Design Engineer **(March 1990 to May 1992)**

▸ Received a two year overview of project management, manufacturing and machining, and quality control at Harris Products through formal course work and hands-on training in the production facilities and engineering design departments.

- Assisted in the machine shop learning operation of shop equipment. Acquired knowledge in design techniques to utilize cost effective machining operations.
- Designed modifications to single and dual terminator pneumatic bench tooling for termination and continuity testing of modular plugs.
- **Patented the TechTron L1-11 Tool design: Patent # 1234567, Feb. 1992.**

Education

Drexel University - Philadelphia, Pennsylvania
Bachelor of Science in Mechanical Engineering - Graduate, 1989
Continuing Education:

- Manufacturing Technologies
- AUTOCAD Rev. 14
- Finite Element Methods
- Medusa Advanced 2-D
- Statistical Engineering
- Quality Control
- Ergonomics
- Timeline
- Lotus/Excel

Supplemental Information

Willing to travel and relocate.

Using the Computer to Land a Job

Scanning for Substance

"Electronics is changing the whole employment game," according to Joyce Lain Kennedy, nationally syndicated careers columnist and author.

"There are at least 30 on-line career services," says Kennedy. Marion C. Evans's resume (which appears in Kennedy's book, *Electronic Resume Revolution*) is an example of an electronic resume that potential employers can scan, store and/or print out.

Since applicants can be sorted by words or categories found in the resume, Evans made sure she included key words so that she would be matched as often as possible. She also selected nouns that are likely to be sorted, rather than concentrate on the traditional action verbs, which will not match any criteria from potential future bosses.

Kennedy also notes that Evans includes all her professional affiliations, even though she doesn't indicate a leadership role in any one of them. "Nevertheless," says Kennedy, "the key words in each organization may result in a computer pulling her name to a computer screen."

Other key points for writing an electronic resume, according to Kennedy, include the following:

- Be sensitive to what a scanner can and cannot do: Don't underline. Skip the use of italics or boldface type. Avoid decorative or other uncommon typefaces. Use white or beige paper. Avoid graphics and shading.
- Minimize the use of general abbreviations (except for more common ones like BA or BS), but maximize the use of industry jargon (MIS, etc.).
- Put your name on the first line; place contact information on a separate line.
- Use white space. Computers love it.
- Use common language to maximize the number of matches.

Joyce Lain Kennedy

Joyce Lain Kennedy is the senior author of *Electronic Job Search Revolution* and *Electronic Resume Revolution* (John Wiley & Sons). Her latest book, *Hook Up, Get Hired!* (John Wiley & Sons), appeared in 1995. Kennedy is also a nationally syndicated columnist on the topic of careers.

MARION C. EVANS
35 Robins Nest Drive
Toledo, OH 53446
419 765-0123

KEYWORDS

Marketing Manager. Buyer. Merchandising Manager. Marketing. Product Development. Promotions. Advertising. Graphics Production. Direct Mail. Media. New Product Introduction. Training. Travel. Wholesale. Bachelor of Arts. Michigan State.

SUMMARY

A marketing manager with in-depth merchandising and product development experience. Employers describe me as a money maker ... and a creative, high-energy problem solver. Excellent at defining and meeting market needs.

PROFESSIONAL EXPERIENCE

TALENT PROFESSIONAL INTERNATIONAL, Cincinnati, OH 1988 to Present
Marketing Manager
Overall creative and financial responsibility to manage and direct four key areas: Wholesale and related businesses, promotions, advertising, visual display, merchandising, and graphics production.

- Created wholesale division product line and systems.
- Doubled company income in three years.
- Initiated and executed in-house graphics production ... saved $150K advertising agency fees annually.
- Executed 1991 corporate image change ... including visual display, retail packaging and promotions.

THE JEFFERSON MINT, Jefferson Center, PA, 1986 - 1988
Program Manager
Developed original artwork in fine porcelain, bronze and pewter from initial concept to direct mail and media promotion. 26 programs plus Christmas catalog each in excess of $2 million in sales. Travel 50% of job.

MILANO CORPORATION, Chicago, IL, 1984 - 1986
Buyer for leading giftware importers
Purchased 20% of company volume. Developed products from idea conception to market placement. Selected product assortments for catalog. Trained national sales force in marketing new product introductions. Traveled extensively overseas, 5 countries, 28 suppliers.

MICHEALS CREATIVE CRAFTS, Chicago, IL, 1983 - 1984
Buyer for 52 stores in 23 national markets
Responsibilities included annual budget programs for sales, inventory and profit. Created total concept, product assortments and systems for the custom frame, organizer and stationery shops. Member of new store and operating committee. Lots of travel.

CRAFTY CRAFTS AND HOBBIES, Northbrook, IL, 1978 - 1983
National Merchandising Manager and Buyer for mid-western chain of 12 stores. Turnkey responsibility to open 7 stores. Selected products for institutional catalog. Lots of travel.

EDUCATION

Bachelor of Arts, Michigan State University, 1972
Numerous Professional Seminars; details upon request.

PROFESSIONAL AFFILIATIONS

American Management Association
Women in Management
American Society of Interior Designers
Hobby Industry Association of America

OTHER

Arts, theater, swimming, needlework, music, dance,
painting, photography, power walking, travel

Power Resume Tip

If you have had little or no work experience or are returning to the job market after an absence, be sure to include any volunteer experience, social responsibilities or charitable activities on your resume. Employers are interested in people who are "doers," regardless of monetary compensation.

A Change in Direction

Emphasizing Experience Related to New Goals

After five years in the work force, Kristen Harris was ready for a career change.

"Since graduating college, Kristen held three jobs in the fields of systems programming and analysis," said Julie Adair King, president and owner of Julie King Creative, Inc. and author of *The Smart Woman's Guide to Resumes and Job Hunting* and *The Smart Woman's Guide to Interviewing and Salary Negotiation*.

"In all three jobs, one of Kristen's responsibilities was to train company employees on how to use various computer systems. This experience caused her to rethink her original long-term goal, which was to be an MIS department manager. She so enjoyed the teaching aspects of her jobs that she decided to move into the training field. There's an opening for a systems trainer in her company, and she's going to apply."

As a result, Kristen created a Skills Summary that emphasizes her training background. "In addition," notes King, "she makes a point to include the fact that she performed training in all of her positions."

The systems trainer position for which she is applying requires a broad knowledge of many different types of hardware, software and programming languages, so Kristen includes a list of those systems in which she is proficient.

Julie Adair King
President, Julie King Creative, Inc.

Julie Adair King is co-author of *The Smart Woman's Guide to Resumes and Job Hunting* and author of *The Smart Woman's Guide to Interviewing and Salary Negotiation*. King is president and owner of Julie King Creative, Inc., a marketing and creative services corporation based in Indianapolis. She frequently talks about career and job hunting issues on radio and TV and leads workshops and lectures. King is also a contributing writer to various publications.

KRISTEN B. HARRIS
3234 Seneca Drive
Houston, TX 77082
(713) 555-2310

Skills Summary

Five years experience in system analysis and programming for international transportation and energy corporations. Strong background in user training and support documentation. Experience in major programming languages, operating hardware and software.

Experience

8/92-present Global Airlines, Houston

Senior Systems Analyst, Sales Administration and Program Development.
Created database programming to meet management and field-sales information needs.

- Design and implement sales systems at company's regional technical centers.
- Train sales staff on use of new programs.
- Developed voice-automation system that increased telemarketing department productivity and allowed 15% staffing reduction.

6/89-8/92 World Oil Company, Houston

Purchasing Systems Analyst, Corporate Procurement and Materials Management.
Promoted from Systems Analyst position in June 1991.
Programmed management-reporting systems for purchasing department.

- Served as liaison between system users and technical support group.
- Trained field systems users.
- Created invoice-reconciliation program that resulted in capturing an average of $5,000 per month in vendor overcharges.

Systems Analyst, Computer Services Organization, June 1989 to June 1991
Designed and implemented systems for crude-oil acquisition applications.
Performed system maintenance programming.

- Wrote computer system procedure specifications and user manuals.
- Designed and supervised programming of tracking system that determined more cost-effective transportation routes.

Systems Proficiency

Hardware: IBM 3090, MVS Operating System/JES2, IBM PS/2 Model 55
Programming Languages: NATURAL/ADABAS, JCL, SAR, SAS, FOCUS, QMF/SQL with DB2, UCC7, ROSCOE, TSO, ISPF, Predict, COBOL, BASIC, PL/1, IBM ASSEMBLER
PC Software: DBase III+, LOTUS Release 3, Harvard Graphics, LOTUS Freelance Plus, DOS, PCTools, PC Focus

Education

1989 B.S., Business Administration/Management Information Systems
Bowling Green State University, Bowling Green, Ohio, 3.7/4.0 GPA

Short On Words, Long On Accomplishments

Getting to the Heart of the Matter

Reading this resume, one definitely gets the impression that this candidate can sell, sell, sell. The recognition she's received from her two most recent employers jumps off the page to a hiring manager looking for a sales person who can really produce.

Ellen Lerner, Certified Personnel Consultant, was attracted to this resume because of its "successful melding of several resume formats" including chronological and functional. Lerner notes that this resume "leaves the reader with a clear picture of the candidate's accomplishments and skills."

"There are not extra words, paragraphs or descriptive sentences," notes Lerner. "Bold type and ample white space are used to direct the reader's eye."

Lerner also appreciated that this candidate featured her accomplishments by using bullets. In addition, "nothing is repeated and irrelevant. Interesting, earlier experience is downplayed, but nonetheless provided in abbreviated form."

Lynn Levy's brief explanation of the hiatus in her career from 1970 to 1981 is one that employers will immediately understand. Had she been involved in volunteer activities during that time, she might have chosen to highlight some of her accomplishments during that period. But, as Lerner notes, "it's best to leave out information that does not help convince employers that you're the best candidate for the job."

"Even after only a brief scanning of this resume, the reader is left with a positive impression that this candidate is indeed a winner."

Ellen Lerner, CPC

Ellen Lerner, Certified Personnel Consultant, is a writer, trainer and former president of Lerner International, Maryland. Before starting her own company in July 1990, she was the director of the hotel division for Roth Young Personnel.

Lerner International was the only executive recruitment firm considered specialists in the professional meeting planning and hotel sales and marketing industries.

An accomplished writer, Lerner has had articles published in *The Meeting Manager* and a variety of association newsletters. She presently writes a regularly featured career column for *Meetings & Conventions*.

Committed to shifting people's orientation from *crisis management* to *professional career management*, she has written and delivered the master career series nationally.

LYNN LEVY
25 Mayflower Court
Westminster, MD 21208
410-555-4849

Employment

2/85-1/92 **SALES REPRESENTATIVE** — TRIA, New York, NY
(The Research Institute of America)

- 1987 - Member - Most Improved Region
- 1988 - Member - Region of the Year
- 1989 - National Representative of the Month
- 1985-1991 - Winner of every incentive contest

Sold professional libraries to accountants, lawyers and corporations in the fields of tax, estate planning, real estate, pensions, benefits, employment and discrimination. Territory included Baltimore City (south to Crofton, Md.).

1981-1985 **SALES MANAGER** — Cooper Dental Laboratory, Baltimore, Md.

- 1982-1984 - #1 sales representative in company
- 1983 - Promoted to manager

* Initiated outside sales
* Newsletter production
* Client seminars
* Direct mail
* Telemarketing
* Client liaison
* Wrote marketing plan

1970-1981 Family responsibilities

1966-1970 Group Therapist at North Charles General Hospital
Vice President, V.M. Real Estate, Inc.
Social Worker for the Department of Social Services, Baltimore
Cook County Hospital, Chicago.

Education

1966 B.A. Sociology, University of Maryland

A Good Presentation Despite Lack of Experience

A Demonstration of Commitment and Interests

Perhaps those candidates who have the most difficulty writing their resumes are candidates who don't yet have on-the-job experience.

Faced with this dilemma, Sam Jones, the candidate whose resume appears on the opposite page, chose not to "snow" prospective employers, as so many candidates in his position do. Instead, he "highlights his education, the skills relating to his area of interest, related work experience and special information on awards," points out Susan M. Gordon. She is president of Lynne Palmer Executive Recruitment, Inc., a New York-based firm specializing in the communications field.

Knowing full well that in publishing he would probably have to launch his career in a clerical position, Jones chose not to include an Objective, which undoubtedly would have appeared presumptuous.

Instead, this resume, "clearly positions his areas of interest in graphic arts and design," says Gordon. "His internship suggests that he is ambitious and hardworking. And his education background at prestigious schools, along with two excellent awards, suggests that he has a great deal of talent."

Lynne Palmer Executive Recruitment, Inc.

Lynne Palmer Executive Recruitment, Inc., is a personnel recruiting firm specializing in the communications area—books and magazines. The company was established in 1964 and serves the publishing industry nationwide on all levels (entry-level to executive).

SAM JONES
123 Amber Street
Jefferson City, Missouri 65107

EDUCATION	B.A. French Language & Literature Photography University of Missouri, May 1992 University of Paris, Sorbonne 1990-1991
SKILLS	• Desktop publishing—Quark XPress, and Pagemaker • Photography—B & W and Color darkroom knowledge
SELECTED WORK EXPERIENCE	
10/91 - Present	ABC Magazine—Production Intern • Trafficking ads through various stages • Clerical Assistant to V.P., Production • Work with desktop publishing system
9/90 - 5/91	University of Missouri, School of Art Responsible for aiding students with use of software for graphic design class
AWARDS & PUBLICATIONS	
	• Finalist, 1992 Photography Award • Tom Jay Award, 1991, for Photography
LANGUAGES	French, Italian

How to Beat 3,000-to-1 Odds

A Job-Winning Resume

"There are two significant attributes that help make this a top-notch resume," says Don Nelson of Superior Advertising of Brooklyn Center, Minnesota.

"One is the format. In the prequalifying round, most resumes receive only about 10 seconds of attention. The format of this resume summarizes and bullet points key qualifications to grab the reader's attention.

"Second," Nelson continues, "this resume is a results-oriented resume, keying on accomplishments that specifically distinguish Michael Davis in the marketplace."

Nelson points out that this resume went up against 3,000 other applicants—and won! The employer commented that this resume was "attention-grabbing." It got Davis the interview. And the interview got Davis the job.

Don Nelson
President, Superior Advertising, Inc.

Don Nelson is the founder and president of Superior Advertising, Inc., a marketing and advertising company that caters to the individual needs of each client. With more than 14 years of extensive experience preparing more than 30,000 results-oriented resume presentations, Superior has the expertise and track record to specifically distinguish anyone in today's competitive marketplace.

MICHAEL J. DAVIS

7000 Brooklyn Boulevard, #202 • Minneapolis, Minnesota 55429

(612) 555-2596

SUMMARY:

A track record of outstanding buying performance in various sophisticated retail environments. Management ability emphasizes problem solving, project coordination, strategic planning and sales/profit integrity. An adept analyst of diverse areas such as purchasing, inventory management, negotiations and sales results analysis.

HIGHLIGHT OF QUALIFICATIONS:

- **Buying/Negotiations**
- **Inventory Management**
- **Market/ Sales Analysis**
- **Procurement Terms**
- **Planning/Organizing**
- **Employee Training**
- **Product Sales/Marketing**
- **Customer Service**

PROFESSIONAL EXPERIENCE:

BUYER, *MNO Software*, October 1991 - Present — Plymouth, MN

- Accountable for department yearly volume of $30 million consisting of hardware, supplies, accessories, and CPU's.
- Responsible for buying/negotiating programs to suit mall based retail margin of a 240 store chain.
- Successful in developing new sources and managing monthly open-to-buy.
- Expedite flow of merchandise to maximize turns ratio and control inventory.
- Handle the sourcing of all product in related areas; negotiate vendor coop programs and dollar amounts.
- Analyze sales results and perform adjustments to maximize results.
- Proof all advertising for area of responsibility; participate in trade shows and manufacturing tours.

Accomplishments:

- Successful in implementing and executing a department turnaround, streamlining all buying operations and exceeding all department goals within 6 months.
- Instrumental in exceeding maximum turns ratio for hardware, supplies, and accessories.
- Key player in increasing overall department productivity by 200%.

ASSISTANT BUYER, *PQR Computer Systems*, October 1989 - October 1991 — Edina, MN

- Responsible for buying of components, supplies and print material for a computer manufacturer with gross sales over $200 million.
- Responsibilities included procuring inventory consistent with forecasted production schedules, negotiating prices and returns, shipping and receiving, coordinating inventory with 3 retail stores, and developing new buying sources.

MERCHANDISE ASSISTANT, *STU Companies Inc.*, August 1988 - October 1989 — Plymouth, MN

ASSISTANT STORE MANAGER, *VWX Company*, September 1987 - August 1988 — Plymouth, MN

DEPARTMENT MANAGER, *YZ Incorporated*, January 1986 - August 1987 — Minneapolis, MN

EDUCATION:

UNIVERSITY OF MINNESOTA — Minneapolis, MN

Bachelor of Science Degree

Triple Major: Management, Marketing and Industrial Relations

Minors: Speech Communications and Economics

Personal and professional references available upon request.

No Bull and Plenty of Bullets

A Resume That Dazzles the Reader With Facts

Read this resume through and see if you notice that anything is missing.

Odds are, you probably *didn't* notice that there is no section labeled Education. Why? Because Eugene D. Thompson, a highly capable candidate in most other respects, never attended college. Therefore, he omitted an Education section because "there's simply no reason to bring up a weakness," says Kenneth Newton, cofounder and principal of Transition Associates in Richmond, Virginia. "Under no circumstances, however, can a resume contain *false* information, including rearranging of dates."

"The resume is designed to *sell* the candidate, not give the employer a reason *not* to buy." Newton uses this resume as an example of the "general concepts" he believes should apply to all resumes.

"It uses a Summary rather than an Objective. I believe that an objective is either so general as to be meaningless or so specific that it can exclude the writer from consideration for related positions.

"In addition, the emphasis is on accomplishments, rather than on duties. People are not hired for *what* they do as much as they are for how *well* they do it."

What's more, these accomplishments are in numeric and percentage terms. "Who would not be attracted to someone who reduced an operating budget by 11 percent or increased profitability of a subsidiary by $3.5 million in one year?"

Kenneth Newton
Cofounder, Principal, Transition Associates

Transition Associates, located in Richmond, Virginia, specializes in corporate outplacement and individual career consulting. Kenneth Newton's background includes a career in professional recruiting and in training in interpersonal communications. He is a charter member of the International Association of Outplacement Professionals.

EUGENE D. THOMPSON

1060 Route 1
Ashland, KY 41101
H - 606-555-1234
W - 606-555-7890

SUMMARY: A professional manager with experience in administration and technical coordination of insurance claim functions for multiple branch offices.

EXPERIENCE:

Williams Holdings, an American International Division

3/88 - Present — NATIONAL CLAIM DIRECTOR. Ashland, KY

- Responsible for supervising home office claims and four claim service offices for this excess and surplus lines insurance carrier.
- Developed and implemented the first complete corporate technical and procedures claim manual, including time and service standards for file reporting and improving the quality of service to policyholders.
- Reduced operating budget by 11%.
- Achieved a 50% reduction in outstanding cases in litigation over two years.

Commercial Insurance Company

1962 - 1988 — REGIONAL CLAIM MANAGER. Harrisburg, PA (2/81 - 3/88)

- Technical and personnel responsibilities for regional claim activities and six branch claim offices in the mid-Atlantic states.
- Achieved a 60% reduction in outstanding claim files.
- Increased the income to Commercial Life Insurance, a subsidiary of Commercial Insurance Company, from $0 to $3.5 million a year by utilizing structured settlements in settlement of casualty claims.
- Reduced staffing from 165 to 118 with no adverse effect on the quality of claim service.
- Reduced the use of independent adjusters on claims from 12% to 1%.

ASSISTANT TERRITORIAL DIRECTOR, HOME OFFICE CLAIMS. New York, NY (1979 - 81)

- Responsible for quality control program and home office audit program for 40 offices countrywide.
- Conducted an average of two home office audits in the field offices per month.

BRANCH CLAIM MANAGER. Springfield, MO (1969 - 79)

- Responsible for the management, technical claim handling and training of claim personnel to handle all lines of claims for the four counties in western Missouri.
- The youngest person to be appointed to the position of Claim Manager at the time of promotion.
- One of two persons selected from the claim department by the company countrywide to become Assistant Branch Manager in charge of underwriting and loss control functions.
- Developed five supervisors who were selected for promotion to Claim Manager in other offices.

BRANCH CLAIM SUPERVISOR. Hamden, CT (1965 - 69)

- Responsible for direct supervision and development of four adjusters handling all lines of property and casualty claims.

OUTSIDE CLAIM ADJUSTER. Hamden, CT (1962 - 65)

- Responsible for handling all lines of claims as an outside adjuster in the assigned territory.

New Hampshire Insurance Company

1960 - 1962 HOME OFFICE PROPERTY CLAIM EXAMINER. Manchester, NH

Peerless Insurance Company

1958 - 1960 JUNIOR FIRE UNDERWRITER. Keene, NH

AFFILIATIONS:

Member - Excess and Surplus Lines Claim Association
Past President - Claim Managers Council

Power Resume Tip

Keep in mind that prospective employers will spend less than 30 seconds reviewing your resume. You must keep it clear, concise and focused on the information that will sell you best.

Every Resume Tells a Story

Letting the Real You Shine Through

Its highly readable and effective job descriptions are what attracted Murray B. Parker to this resume. Parker is founder and president of The Borton Wallace Company, a retained search consultancy in the pulp and paper industry based in Asheville, North Carolina. For instance, this candidate, James Rogers, has clearly laid out his career in chronological order, listing each position, describing the nature and scope of environment and *briefly* explaining his accountabilities.

This establishes a frame of reference for the most important part of his resume, the Key Accomplishments. Here, James is able to clearly spell out his impact on the business. Not his activities, but his results. What he accomplished is stated in easy-to-understand specific terms such as dollars saved annually or percentage of improvement. These are the claims that will make a prospective employer sit up and take notice.

Note, too, that despite all of the description, the candidate has designed the resume with a terrific amount of white space, making it highly readable and scannable.

"This resume tells the candidate's story most effectively, clearly and in the shortest space possible," says Parker. "After all, with a resume it's important to be clear and easy to read, yet answer all the key questions an employer might have."

Murray B. Parker
Founder and President, The Borton Wallace Company

Murray B. Parker is a charter member and director of the National Association of Executive Recruiters and a member of the Technical Association of Pulp & Paper Industry. He generated two patents and several million pounds-per-year products while at DuPont, then pursued a petroleum products new venture before embarking on his professional recruiting career.

Founded in 1978, The Borton Wallace Company is a retained search consultancy focused on technical and operations functions within the pulp and paper and supplier industries.

JAMES ROGERS

55 Silver Court
Mallard, MD 21178

Home: (301) 555-7275
Office: (301) 555-6345

OBJECTIVE: Challenging operations management position at the corporate, division, or business unit level where broad management skills in operations management can be fully utilized.

PROFESSIONAL HIGHLIGHTS:

1989 to Present **SOFT SPRITZ CORPORATION, COLLEGE PARK, MD**

Group Plant Manager, Silver Springs, MD **(10/89 to Present)**
Report to Division Operations Manager of this $5 billion, Fortune 200, beverage and fast foods company. Full P&L responsibility for management of $50 million budget, 15 million unit, 140 employee soft drink bottling operation. Functional accountabilities include production operations, plant engineering, warehousing, distribution, and quality control.

Key Accomplishments:

- **Directed successful $2 million redesign/rebuild of manufacturing facility (annual savings $700 thousand).**

- **Reduced workforce by 28% through reconfiguration of bottling line and warehouse methods improvement (annual savings $400 thousand).**

- **Created task force that reduced product "shrinkage" by 85% (annual savings $425 thousand).**

- **Initiated "driver assist" program reducing warehouse loading crew by 30% and overtime hours by 8 thousand per year (annual savings $220 thousand).**

Acquisitions/Special Projects Manager **(1/89-10/89)**
College Park, MD
Reported to Vice President of Operations.
Responsible for directing the smooth transition of 3 newly acquired franchise bottling plants into the Soft Spritz corporate plant network environment. Directed activities of 3 plant managers in installation of administrative systems that resulted in significantly improved operating results.

Key Accomplishments:

- **Led corporate headquarters staff team in the development of a strategic model to guide all future business expansion and site selection.**

- **Directed "sourcing needs" study of Western Region resulting in shutdown of** bottling facility ($800 thousand annual savings).

- Directed warehouse consolidation project in Western Region, consolidating 3 high cost warehouses into 1 new strategically located facility ($800 thousand annual savings).

- Initiated labor control reports allowing management to eliminate wasted manpower (annual savings $200 thousand).

1975 to 1989 **FAMOUS BEVERAGE COMPANY, PITTSBURGH, PA**

Plant Manager, Pittsburgh, PA (1985-1989)
Reported to Division Operations Manager. Directed staff of 5 with full P&L responsibility for operation of 2 bottling plants (190 employees, 15 million units, $45 million budget). Functional accountability for production, maintenance, warehousing, and quality.

Key Accomplishments:

- Served on Board of Directors of Wilson Packaging Cooperative (1981-1989) with significant improvement to operating results (annual savings $1.5 million).

- Reduced overall operating costs by 31% while increasing production volume by 19%.

- Directed successful installation of $5 million bottling equipment resulting in 25% reduction in headcount (annual savings $1.1 million).

Plant Manager, Beaver, PA (1980-1985)
Reported to Division Operations Manager. Full P&L responsibility for 160 employee, $40 million, 9 million unit soft drink bottling operation.

Plant Manager III, Detroit, MI (1979-1980)
Reported to Division Operations Manager with P&L responsibility for 100 employee, 4 million unit bottling operation (annual budget $20 million).

Production Manager, Detroit, MI (1978-1979)

Ass't Production Manager, Detroit, MI (1975-1978)

EDUCATION: B.S., Engineering, University of Michigan
Major: Mechanical Engineering

REFERENCES: Excellent referenced available upon request.

Power Resume Tip

Spotlight your most important sales points. Your most impressive and relevant qualifications should be highlighted with boldface type or other design elements, so they will be immediately apparent to someone scanning your resume.

When a Functional Resume Makes Sense

For a Candidate Who Didn't Follow a Traditional Path

"A functional resume such as Ellen Azevedo's is particularly effective for candidates whose important work skills were acquired outside the usual full-time employment environment," says Louis Persico. He is founder and president of Career Management Consultants, Inc.

"Although many experts advise against using a functional resume format, it is a useful tool for people making career changes or for those who need to highlight skills and achievements they've developed away from work."

Persico points out that Ellen Azevedo's resume was key in her securing a position as a publications editor for a leading trade association although she hadn't worked full-time for 16 years. "She had developed most of the skills she needed for the position through volunteer work, irregular freelance assignments and part-time work. The functional format was particularly helpful during her networking interviews because the listing of her capability areas stood out visually and could be understood at a glance."

Persico explains, "All resumes are sales documents. They are brochures designed to demonstrate value to the potential buyer (employer). In deciding what information to include, job seekers should ask if the information demonstrates experience, skills, knowledge or personality traits that would have value to a potential employer.

"The bottom-line criterion for inclusion of information revolves around value and includes performance. Thus, the functional resume should list not only what the candidate has done, but how well he or she has done it."

Although Azevedo's resume demonstrates almost nothing in the way of traditional job experience, it does demonstrate skills that an employer looking for a skilled communicator would desire.

Louis Persico
Founder, President, Career Management Consultants, Inc.

Louis Persico is founder and president of Career Management Consultants, Inc., a firm providing corporate-sponsored outplacement and individual career transition services. As the oldest firm of its kind in Harrisburg, PA, CMC offers a full range of individual and group outplacement programs, customized to meet the needs of clients and sponsoring companies.

An important service of CMC is the quarterly, "Career Outplacement Newsletter," published by Persico and edited by Kate Duttro, D.Ed., freelance writer on business, career and cross-cultural topics. Several articles that originally appeared in the newsletter have been reprinted for other publications including *The Wall Street Journal's National Business Employment Weekly*.

ELLEN AZEVEDO

40 Blue Ridge Road
Lancaster, PA 17601
(717) 555-1111

OBJECTIVE: A program coordinator or public relations position requiring creativity with refined oral/written communicating, organizing and instructing skills.

QUALIFICATIONS: Solid experience in initiating, implementing and promoting agency programs. Successful free-lance writing experience.

CAPABILITY AREAS: SPECIFIC RELATED ACCOMPLISHMENTS

PUBLIC RELATIONS: Researched functions, needs and goals of 4 social service agencies. Wrote/edited newsletters and brochures. Publications cited by boards and staffs for contributions to public image and fund raising.

COMMUNICATING: Successfully researched and wrote 40 human interest articles published in 9 major regional and national publications including Jamestown Enquirer (circ. 323,000) and Working Parent (circ. 220,000).

Co-authored 175-page novel praised by Penguin Publishing Co. executive editor for "good writing and perceptive characterization."

ORGANIZING: Perceived need for Episcopal parish. Recruited members, procured meeting place and convened meetings. Served as elected lay leader for 3 years, overseeing all committees. By end of term, congregation had purchased and renovated a church building and hired a pastor.

Started church-based Central America committee. Organized and presented recruitment programs, obtained sponsorship and acted as liaison with other groups. Coordinated letter writing campaigns and initiated Guatemalan sister parish relationship. Committee's vibrancy/commitment recognized in annual parish report.

INSTRUCTING: Designed and conducted college level writing course for an industrial setting. Secured supplemental materials and fashioned course around Grapes of Wrath. Received high student evaluations for creativity and interest.

Initiated and taught high school creative writing course and published first literary magazine. Commended by department head for organization and teaching ability.

EXPERIENCE: Free-lance Writer, 1984 - Present.

Real Estate Broker, Jonesville, Iowa, 1981 - 1983.

Adjunct Writing Instructor, Jonesville University, Jonesville, Iowa, 1976 - 1979.

English Teacher, 1969 - 1976.

OTHER EXPERIENCE: Consultant, Brochure Development, Family Children's Center, Lancaster, PA, 1988.

Consultant, Editorial and Public Relations, Sunshine Youth Home, Westville, Idaho, 1987.

EDUCATION: M.A.T., Education (major field, English)
Temple University, Philadelphia, PA, 1974

B.S. Education
Temple University, Philadelphia, PA, 1969
GPA: 3.3

ADDITIONAL SKILLS: Word Processing

Power Resume Tip

You may want to mention any unique educational experience you've had, such as spending a year as a foreign exchange student, or an intern. Even if these experiences aren't directly linked to your career goal, they indicate that you are a person who is open to new opportunities and challenges.

Tell Recruiters What They Want to Hear

A Resume That's a Perfect Combination

Here's a resume written in the combination format that works extraordinarily well to highlight the candidate's skills and experiences.

"I like this resume since it demonstrates a very important point: Candidates should tell the recruiters *exactly what they want to hear*," relates David A. Pizzuti, employee development specialist with the Public Service Company of Colorado, based in Denver.

"Mark Wasson sent me this resume in response to an advertisement I had placed in the local newspapers for a communications officer. The ad listed the requirements that I felt were essential for the qualified candidate to possess.

"This resume not only addressed the job requirements that I had listed, but it also went so far as to present them in the exact order they appeared in the ad!"

Pizzuti noted that he reviews an average of 150 to 200 resumes per job opening. "Therefore, I am not able to spend a great deal of time searching for an applicant's qualifications. This resume enabled me to see easily that this applicant did indeed possess all of the qualifications, without my having to 'read between the lines.' "

One particularly interesting feature of this resume is that the format allowed the candidate to freely intermingle his volunteer and professional work experience, thus amplifying the credibility of his claims to expertise in so broad a range of disciplines.

David A. Pizzuti
Employee Development Specialist,
Public Service Company of Colorado

The Public Service Company of Colorado is a medium-sized utility company providing gas, electric and steam power to customers throughout Colorado and Wyoming. As a member of the Human Resource Division, David A. Pizzuti has a background in recruitment, outplacement and employee development for all levels of the company. He also presents job preparation and resume writing workshops for various nonprofit agencies, colleges and military bases throughout Denver.

MARK J. WASSON
550 15TH STREET
DENVER, CO 80202
(303)555-8531

CAREER OBJECTIVE: Corporate Communications Officer.

EDUCATION: Graduated 1987 from University of Colorado, Cum Laude,Degree in Marketing with a Business Administration Minor.

SKILLS INVENTORY

MARKETING: Co-wrote demand survey for Adams County Economic Development Council, interviewed 5% of sample, analyzed surveys, wrote and presented report on findings, for the purpose of developing business retention strategies. Write and edit copy, design and layout, of sales flyers, brochures and display ads. Design, price, and purchase giveaway items such as pens, mugs, etc. Coordinate marketing efforts of mortgage company with affiliated builder including newspaper advertising, community relations.

EVENTS PLANNING: Planned and coordinated 1991 and 1992 National Branch Managers Meetings for mortgage company including; travel arrangements, hotel and accommodations selections, social functions, agenda, and presentation schedule. Committee Chair, Cherry Creek Arts Festival -- 1991 Chair, Artist Demonstrations (10 volunteers), 1992 Co-Chair, Volunteer Coordination (950 volunteers); recruit, train and direct volunteers, deliver committee reports to board, verbal presentations at volunteer rallies and training sessions, final report to festival director.

RESEARCH AND WRITING: Volunteer research assistant, Adams County Economic Development Council; Volunteer research assistant, Denver Minority Business Development Center; Oil and gas prospect and reserve research resulting in feasibility reports; Sales flyers and brochures; Ad copy; Personnel handbooks; Proposals; Corporate minutes; Business correspondence.

COMPUTER: IBM PC XT, Macintosh; Lotus 1-2-3 2.2, WordPerfect 5.0, Quark Xpress, Harvard Graphics, Patton, Microsoft Word, AS-400, NBI, System 38, OGRE, ECARRS; Pascal.

MANAGEMENT: Interview, hire, train and review clerical personnel; Recruit, direct and review 950-1000 volunteers as committee co-chair for Cherry Creek Arts Festival; Train managers on policy, procedures and reporting; Coordinate paper flow for hiring, reviewing and personnel reporting for corporation; Provide training on Americans with Disabilities Act.

FINANCIALS: Evaluate annual reports, income statements, balance sheets; Understand corporate financial planning concepts; A/P, A/R payroll, taxes, reconciliations; Construction project accounting; Submitted billings to federal agencies and maintained billing systems.

M. Wasson page 2

WORK HISTORY:

April 1990 to Present	Cherry Creek Arts Festival, Non-Profit Organization for the Arts 1991, Chair, Artist Demonstrations Committee 1992, Co-Chair Volunteer Coordination
August 1987 to Present	**MCD Holdings, Inc.** Corporate Communications Specialist
July 1985 to August 1987	**Bantom Exploration,** Public Relations Assistant

PROFESSIONAL REFERENCES AND WRITING SAMPLES AVAILABLE UPON REQUEST.

Power Resume Tip

The best method for producing your resume is to use a personal computer to create it and a high-quality computer printer to reproduce it. This will allow you to make changes instantly, and easily update or modify it to respond to specific job opportunities.

Take Flight From the Pigeonhole

A Resume That Acts as a Change Agent

"This candidate's objective was to change careers," notes Lauri Ann Plante, professional services consultant for Right Associates in Philadelphia. "Therefore, a functional resume was his best option for highlighting accomplishments that he gained from work and nonwork experiences.

"A chronological resume," continues Plante, "would have pigeonholed this person in a field he no longer wished to be in and would not have clearly identified his other strengths."

Steven J. Company achieved his money-management know-how strictly by handling his own finances and working with friends and family. His work experience had no relation to what he now saw as his career goal, which is stated clearly in his Objective paragraph.

"Notice how his professional affiliation helps validate his credentials as a highly motivated, well-organized business leader," points out Plante. "His accomplishments are enough to whet the appetite of any prospective employer."

Lauri Ann Plante
Professional Services Consultant, Right Associates

At Right Associates, Lauri Plante is responsible for managing the professionals on the firm's project staff team. A human resources professional with more than 15 years' experience, primarily in financial services, Plante's career emphasis has been in recruitment and employee relations at both field and corporate levels. In addition to her work with individual candidates at Right Associates, she has conducted workshops for numerous corporations to assist their employees in career transition.

Prior to joining Right Associates, she implemented the first field human resource function at City Federal Savings and Loan and successfully reduced turnover by 50 percent. Plante pioneered recruitment efforts in a ground-floor operation at the corporate offices of The Traveler's Mortgage Services.

She has been featured in *Who's Who of American Women* and was nominated into *Who's Who of Emerging Leaders*. She is currently president of Tri-State Human Resource Management Association. She is a frequent guest speaker on various career management issues.

STEVEN J. COMPANY

123 XYZ Lane
Medford, NJ 08123
(609) 555-5555

OBJECTIVE

A position in which financial planning skills can be used to help clients increase wealth over the long term through the use of appropriate investment strategies and vehicles.

BACKGROUND

A highly motivated, self-taught personal investment strategist, with ten years of successful results in developing individual financial plans. Well-organized business manager. Well versed and experienced in a broad spectrum of issues in personal money management, including:

- Retirement
- Insurance
- Stocks and bonds
- Short and long range strategies
- Family budgeting
- Savings
- Mutual Funds

PROFESSIONAL ACCOMPLISHMENTS

- Improved personal finances from state of debt to one of substantial net worth, through methodical research, observation, and application of sound investment principles.
- Developed and refined a system of reliable, proven rules for personal investing which avoid common investment mistakes.
- Designed successful investment strategies for individual clients in a wide variety of age brackets and income groups with sensitivity to a diversity of individual goals, priorities and attitudes towards risk.
- Conducted seminars in various aspects of financial planning and investing, as organizer and leader of investment club.
- Consistent reader and student of numerous financial publications.
- Gained reputation for sound, conservative investment counsel, with high success rate of client follow through on advice given.

EMPLOYMENT

THE RETAIL CHAIN, Merion, NJ — **1980 - 1991**

Distribution Center Supervisor

GQC CORPORATION , Princeton, NJ — **1973 - 1980**

Supervisor

BLUE, GREEN & YELLOW PUBLISHING, Austin, TX — **1973**

Crew Chief

EDUCATION

B.A., Political Science
University of Florida, Gainesville, FL

AFFILIATIONS

- Vice Chairman Board of Directors, Junior Achievement
- Chairman of Selective Service Board of Hope County
- Board of Trustees, Congregation of Good People, Medford Lakes, NJ

A Resume Aimed at the Hiring Manager

Go Straight to the Top

While many of the recruitment professionals quoted in this book cite the virtues of one-page resumes, Temple Porter, vice president of the Raleigh Consulting Group, is clearly in the opposite camp.

"The 'one page is best' advice comes not from decision-makers, but from those burdened with screening the things," says Porter. "I advise people not to target the resume screeners at all, to stay out of the paper blizzard where they will be only snowflakes."

Indeed, if a candidate can get around the "paper blizzard," a resume such as this one, which is so complete it almost makes the interview inevitable, might indeed help him convince a hiring manager that he or she should talk to the candidate. Porter says that the resume of Adam Carter makes the relevant information highly accessible, is scannable and contains enough depth to convince the hiring manager of the high caliber of this candidate.

In addition, this resume goes a step beyond most by explaining why the candidate is available. Note the sentence at the end of the resume's first page: "On the heels of the expansion's completion came the inevitable reorganizations, which make a career transition a prudent move for me at this time."

Porter also praises the Areas of Expertise section and the Related Accomplishments list that accompanied this candidate's resume.

"The list is keyed to the probable hot buttons of the hiring decision-maker," says Porter.

Temple Porter, CMC
Vice President, Raleigh Consulting Group, Inc.

In his role as career consultant, Temple Porter oversees corporate outplacement, employee selection assignments, career development programs and career crisis counseling. More than 20 years of experience with some of the most successful organizations in the world form the foundation for Porter's consulting practice. He works with his clients to increase productivity, solidify commitment and develop effective work relationships. Porter's popular management workshops, "Managing Priorities," "Selecting the Right Person (the First Time)" and "Dealing with Difficult Employees" have helped hundreds of managers across the nation increase their personal effectiveness.

ADAM B. CARTER
1234 Rambling Way Drive
East Jarvis, New Mexico 12345
(123) 555-7890

OBJECTIVE Contribute to the continued growth and profitability of a successful manufacturing organization by leading efforts in corporate administration, facilities planning, and operations management.

QUALIFICATION SUMMARY Seventeen years of increasing responsibility and senior level leadership in administrative and manufacturing management with some of the U.S.'s premier pharmaceutical firms.

AREAS OF EXPERTISE

Engineering	Leadership	Corporate admin.
Cost containment	Increased profit	Leadership
Plant operations	Productivity increase	5-yr master planning
Problem solving	U.S. & int'l distribution	Facility management

PROFESSIONAL EXPERIENCE

1979 to 1990 GLAXO, INC., Research Triangle Park, NC
(Subsidiary of Glaxo Holdings, p.l.c., London, U.K.)
Having turned around Mead-Johnson's pharmaceutical packaging organization, I was recruited to Glaxo by Phil Priola (then Executive VP), to expand Glaxo from 50K s.f. ($8MM in revenue) to its current 1.3MM s.f. ($2.5B in revenue).

1983 to present **DIRECTOR OF CORPORATE ADMINISTRATION**
Managed all U.S. production operations. Planned and managed the design and construction of R&D labs, administrative, and maintenance facilities totaling 1.3MM s.f. and accommodating the needs of 4,400 employees. Led the development of the corporation's 5-year master plans for facilities and employees. Created the foundation for Glaxo's volatile growth by developing staff and support functions to serve 4,400 employees in 29 departments. On the heels of the expansion's completion came the inevitable reorganizations, which make a career transition a prudent move for me at this time.

1979 to 1988

GLAXO, INC. (Continued)

DIRECTOR OF ENGINEERING

Negotiated and purchased 400 acres of land, planned, designed, and constructed Glaxo's five corporate administrative buildings (500K s.f.) and master-planned remaining site for expansion of 1.6 million s.f. Negotiated and leased (buy options) for 11 research and development buildings (450K s.f.), and leased and started-up 17 buildings (350K s.f.) throughout the U.S. to support distribution, sales and marketing, and corporate affairs. Provided all maintenance and administrative support for these facilities.

1981 to 1987

DIRECTOR OF DISTRIBUTION

Created the international (computer based) network and transportation system by which Glaxo distributes all its products, including sales and marketing promotional materials and samples. Chaired the New Products Introduction Team and coordinated and launched all products into the U.S. pharmaceutical market. Developed and coordinated the import and export of products and services internationally to insure all corporate product planning strategies were carried out.

1979 to 1981

MANAGER OF U.S. OPERATIONS

Recruited by Glaxo as Manager of U.S. Operations to lead the U.S. team for the selection of sites and facilities for expansion of the parent Glaxo Holdings, p.l.c. (U.K. based) into the U.S. pharmaceutical market. This included research labs, production plants, administrative offices, and the corporate headquarters. Coordinated FDA product approvals (including facility, manufacturing, packaging, and distribution regulations). Managed all production operations and support services and departments for the manufacture and distribution of products for the US market, including FDA compliance of international products.

1975 to 1979

MEAD-JOHNSON, Evansville, IN

PACKAGING MANAGER

Learned of this opportunity from a recruiter, and entered Mead-Johnson as their first "under 25" manager. Was challenged to turn around a packaging department of 200 employees operating $600K/yr over budget, with very high reject/rework rates, and uncontrolled material losses. Led the operations group through the planning, design, construction and start-up of Mead-Johnson Park expansion (250,000 s.f.). Corrected morale problems, reduced reject/rework rate, material losses, and increased productivity 76% (boosting annual profit by $3.6 million).

1973 to 1975	ARMOUR PHARMACEUTICAL, Kankakee, IL **LEAD MANUFACTURING SUPERVISOR** **Entered Armour from college as a shift supervisor in the pharmaceutical manufacturing department. Promoted to Lead Manufacturing Supervisor. Multiple shift responsibilities included leading the department to product yield increases of 17% by improving manufacturing procedures and recovery of discarded product. These improvements resulted in an annual savings of $2.9MM and 6.5% increased plant capacity.**
EDUCATION	B.S., Chemistry, 1973, University of Kentucky, Lexington, KY
PROFESSIONAL DEVELOPMENT	Harvard Business School, 1989 Wharton School of Business, 1987-88 Center for Creative Leadership, 1986-87
PROFESSIONAL AFFILIATIONS	International Facilities Management Association Chambers of Commerce, Raleigh and Durham, NC Executive Committee, Research Triangle Foundation General Contractors Association
COMMUNITY ACTIVITIES	PTA, Athens High School, Raleigh, NC Construction Committee, White Memorial Church Project Graduation, Wake County School System Chairman, Community Awareness Committee
PERSONAL	Born Sept. 2, 1951 6', 170 lbs. Married, one child Competition runner (10,000 meters) Competitive racquetball (tournament player)

Adam B. Carter

Some Related Accomplishments

LEADERSHIP

- Led the effort to introduce UK and U.S. product lines and gain the #2 position in the US pharmaceutical market.
- Built Glaxo's $250 million R&D and administrative campus (1.3MM s.f. accommodating 2,600 employees) in Research Triangle Park, NC.
- Created the foundation for Glaxo's volatile growth by developing staff and support functions to serve 4,400 people in 29 departments.

PROBLEM SOLVING

- Contributed to Glaxo's reputation as U.S.'s premier "customer-responsive" pharmaceutical firm by developing a unique product distribution strategy.
- Gained control of Glaxo's major performance targets in an explosive growth environment by creating term service and employment contracts to supplement planned staffing.

INCREASED PROFITS

- Boosted annual profit $3.6 million by reducing cost per unit 1.8¢ by implementing package design changes and automation of existing packaging equipment.
- Achieved a $4.9 million profit by negotiating long-term facility and equipment lease contracts.

COST CONTAINMENT

- Trimmed $14.8 million from planned capital investment (while remaining on target with all corporate objectives) by negotiating facility, service and employment contracts.
- Reduced distribution costs of products and promotional materials from 2.7% to 1.2% of annual sales by negotiating third-party storage, distribution and transportation contracts.

IMPROVED PRODUCTIVITY

- Increased product yields 17% (resulting in annual savings of $2.9 million) by improving product batch procedures and recovery of discarded product during manufacturing.
- Raised packaging line efficiencies 76% (gaining $1.4 million annually) by restructuring packaging staff, maintenance, and engineering responsibilities, automating existing equipment, and changing package designs.

Power Resume Tip

Use single spacing for individual listings and double space between sections and paragraphs. This divides information into easily digestible doses and wards off the "sea of type" look, which is intimidating and difficult to read.

A Resume That Answers Most Employers' Questions

Clear and Specific Information

No one would ever accuse Kathryn Johnson, whose resume appears over the following four pages, of being an underachiever.

This resume is "incredibly clear and specific," says Barbara L. Provus, the principal and cofounder of Shepherd Bueschel & Provus, Inc.

"Putting the position titles in boldface all-caps ensures that they jump out at you. She provides brief descriptions of the companies, and defines reporting and staff relationships so that the resume reviewer will have a clear idea of her career track and the types of environments in which she worked."

In addition, Johnson lists her accomplishments and responsibilities, keeping the explanations very brief so that they can be easily scanned.

"Kathryn also demonstrates that she was active in—not just a member of—appropriate professional organizations," says Provus.

"There's plenty of data here, but it's all relevant and would definitely be sufficient to determine the individual's technical qualifications for a position."

However, despite her admiration for this resume, Provus has some reservations about it. "I think that it could be a little shorter, particularly if Kathryn had condensed her earlier work experience. I would also suggest the inclusion of information on her professional objectives, ability to relocate, etc. In addition, since this is such a long resume, a summary would have helped ensure that the important information gets noticed."

Barbara Provus

Principal, Cofounder, Shepherd Bueschel & Provus, Inc.

Shepherd Bueschel & Provus, Inc., develops and conducts senior-level executive search assignments for a wide range of major U.S. and multinational corporations.

Previously, Provus was a vice president with a "top ten" international executive search firm; manager of Management Development for Federated Department Stores; and has held several positions in human resources and executive search with Booz•Allen & Hamilton.

Provus is active in several professional and nonprofit associations.

KATHRYN J. JOHNSON
1234 James Street, Chicago, Illinois 60000
(312) 555-4567 (residence)
(312) 555-4321 (business)

EDUCATION

Purdue University, Lafayette, Indiana, B.A., Political Science, 1970, Summa Cum Laude

University of Michigan, Ann Arbor, Michigan, M.A., Library Science, 1974; M.B.A., 1983, Marketing Concentration

EMPLOYMENT HISTORY

GARFIELD CORPORATION
Chicago, Illinois
July 1989 to Present

Garfield Corporation is a manufacturer and distributor of food ingredients. The company serves its 3,000 customers through a network of six plants located throughout the United States. For Fiscal Year 1991, sales were approximately $400 million, with approximately 2,000 employees. The company's common stock is listed and traded on the American Stock Exchange.

VICE PRESIDENT, PUBLIC AFFAIRS

- Reports to Chairman and Chief Executive Officer.
- No staff.
- Responsible for creating, implementing and managing overall corporate communications programs.
- Develops strategy for ongoing communications with investors, the media, and employees designed to present the company's strategies, prospects and activities to its various constituencies:

—Investor Relations

—Maintains contact with security analysts, portfolio managers and security holders.
—Writes, edits and produces annual and quarterly reports to shareholders.
—Arranges and manages meetings with financial community.
—Manages annual meeting; writes speeches for management.

—Media Relations

—Writes and distributes press releases including quarterly and annual earnings announcements, personnel announcements, and new product introductions.
—Handles all media inquiries; arranges interviews with management.
—Serves as company spokesman with financial and trade media.

—Employee Communications

—Writes, edits and produces quarterly employee newsletter.
—Arranges all employee meetings; prepares remarks for management.

—Public Relations

—Writes, edits and produces corporate marketing materials.
—Advises management on public relations activities.
—Writes speeches for and provides communications counsel to management.

- Developed overall corporate communications strategy. Brought "in-house" investor relations and media relations activities previously handled by outside consultants. Resulted in annual savings of $200,000.
- Developed and instituted quarterly employee newsletter.
- Wrote, edited and produced first corporate marketing brochure.
- Wrote executive speeches for analyst meetings, all employee meetings, paper industry conferences, and community, industrial, and development meetings.
- Developed guidelines and program for corporate contributions.
- Wrote, edited and produced marketing brochure on company's recycled products.

CRANSCO FOODS — **DIRECTOR, INVESTOR RELATIONS**
February 1987 to June 1989 — Boise, Idaho

Cransco Foods manufacturers grocery products including cheese, pourable dressings for salads, mayonnaise and salad dressing, barbeque sauce, margarine, condiments, confections and fruit spreads. Annual sales for Cransco were approximately $4.8 billion in 1988, with 12,000 employees. Cransco was acquired by Miller Corp. 1989, at which point the Director, Investor Relations position was eliminated at Cransco.

- Reported to the Vice President of Investor Relations.
- Managed two support staff.
- Responsible for developing and implementing investor relations programs directed toward institutional investors.
- Maintained ongoing communications with analysts and portfolio managers in the U.S. and Europe.
- Wrote speeches, developed multimedia presentations, and prepared financial press releases.
- Analyzed peer group and industry data, prepared reports and recommendations to management on investor-related issues, and monitored trading activity and share ownership in the U.S., Europe and Japan.
- Headed task force formed to advise management on how to increase employee ownership of Cransco stock through modification of the company's thrift plan.
- Managed two-day seminar for 100 security analysts and financial media at which Cransco's most senior executives made presentations.
- Responsibilities included program theme and content, speech and slide preparation, production of collateral pieces, and logistics.
- Served on task force responsible for successfully listing Cransco stock on the Tokyo Stock Exchange; negotiated fees and services with dividend paying agent.
- Implemented new procedures for dissemination of information to security analysts resulting in annual savings of $10,000.
- Updated the investor relations department computer systems resulting in annual savings of $24,000.

MWJ CORPORATION

Denver, Colorado
October 1979 to January 1987

MJW Corporation was a natural resources (oil and gas) company with annual revenues of approximately $900 million.

September 1980 to January 1987 — **DIRECTOR, FINANCIAL RELATIONS**

October 1979 to August 1980 — **ASSISTANT DIRECTOR, FINANCIAL RELATIONS**

- Reported to the Chairman and CEO.
- Managed staff of two.
- Responsible for creating, implementing and managing communications programs directed toward investors, the media, and employees for this $2 billion independent oil and gas company.
- Wrote, edited and produced annual and quarterly reports to shareholders.
- Maintained contact with security analysts and portfolio managers, wrote speeches and prepared slide presentations.
- Served as company spokesman with national and local media and the financial community.
- Provided communications counsel to management.
- Managed investor and media relations during crisis situations, including well explosions, lawsuits, unusual stock trading activity, proxy fights, financial restructurings and tender offers.
- Initiated Investor Reference Guide to explain complicated corporate structure and Company's capabilities to security analysts; initiated Corporate Fact Book as a quick reference for financial and operational statistics.
- Received Nicholson Award for Best in Industry Annual Report from National Association of Investors Corporation.

UNITED STATES SENATE

United States Federal Government

Springfield, Illinois
January 1974 to September 1979

November 1975 to September 1979 — **STAFF AIDE TO U.S. SENATOR JOHN DOE**

- Responsible for scheduling the Senator's activities.
- Prepared agendas, speeches, constituent profiles, background and briefing materials; organized media coverage and press releases.
- Coordinated the Senator's nominations to military academies.
- Performed constituent casework and special project analysis covering Department of State, Justice and HEW.

January 1974 to October 1975 **STAFF ASSISTANT**

- Prepared financial reports filed with Federal Election Commission and Secretary of the Senate for Doe for Senate Campaign Committee.

UNIVERSITY OF KANSAS **LIBRARIAN**
February 1969 to January 1974 Lawrence, Kansas

- Served as liaison for the University library and 1,500 foreign and domestic book dealers.
- Responsible for resolving problems with book orders, monitoring $3 million book budget, authorizing invoice payments, preparing annual acquisition statistics.

PROFESSIONAL AFFILIATIONS

Food Industry Finance Exchange, 1988 to Present

National Investor Relations Institute
Board of Directors, 1984 to 1988
Vice President/Secretary, 1987 to 1988
Vice President/Strategic Planning, 1986 to 1987
Vice President/Membership, 1985 to 1986

Public Relations Society of America, 1980 to 1987

Power Resume Tip

When you summarize your responsibilities, use action words, such as "directed," "created," "implemented," etc., and avoid repeating the same words.

Engineered for High Performance

Just Answer These Three Questions

"What makes this resume so great," said Bill Radin, president of Radin Associates, "is that it answers the three basic questions asked by all employers before a hiring decision can be made:"

1. Does the candidate possess the formal education or special training needed to do the job?
2. Is the candidate's work experience relevant and transferable to the position I need to fill?
3. Is it likely that the candidate will be able to help my company in the future?

"Notice how the candidate describes in explicit detail his educational credentials, computer skills, lab experience and math proficiency, as well as what he's accomplished for his previous employers," says Radin. "Armed with this information, the person reading the resume can easily predict the potential benefits of hiring this candidate."

Radin is a strong believer in the chronological format, particularly for a candidate with good credentials. "A summary or functional resume should never be submitted unless your employment history is choppy or you're in the midst of a career change," he notes.

Further, Radin does not believe it's necessary to include a large number of bells and whistles. "Conspicuously absent in this resume are irrelevant tidbits such as career objectives, personal interests and professional references." In true engineer's fashion, Radin believes that if something doesn't have a function, it shouldn't be included in the design.

Bill Radin
President, Radin Associates

Bill Radin began his career in executive search after receiving his master's degree from the University of Southern California in 1985. He is president of Radin Associates, an executive search firm in Santa Fe, New Mexico, specializing in the placement of engineers and technical professionals. His list of client companies includes such multinational giants as TRW, NEC, Westinghouse, Eaton and Mobil Oil. Radin's highly acclaimed, best-selling books, *Billing Power! The Recruiter's Guide to Peak Performance* and *The Recruiter's Almanac*, have been sold in the United States and seven foreign countries; and his guest column appears regularly in the industry trade magazine *Personnel Consultant*. His latest book, *Breakaway Careers*, was published in 1994.

MICHAEL SHARFE

102 Bethany Avenue
Glen Burnie, MD 21060
(301) 555-4896 (H)
(301) 555-2397 (W)

EDUCATION

MASTER OF SCIENCE, MECHANICAL ENGINEERING. West Virginia Institute of Technology, Montgomery, WV. December 1987. Concentration in Thermal Science and Fluid Mechanics. Thesis topic: ***"Transient Enthalpy Modeling of a Phase Change Heat Storage System."*** Stimulation of system's transient behavior via Finite difference Techniques.

BACHELOR OF SCIENCE, MECHANICAL ENGINEERING. West Virginia Institute of Technology, Montgomery, WV. May 1985

SPECIALIZED TRAINING

FINITE ELEMENT BASED SOFTWARE FOR COMPUTATIONAL FLUID DYNAMICS AND HEAT TRANSFER (FIDAP).

TRAINED AND CERTIFIED IN "QUALITY ENGINEERING BY DESIGN—THE TAGUCHI APPROACH." Design of Experiments Techniques. Rochester Institute of Technology, 1989

EXPERIENCE

<u>R&D Engineer, Bowles Fluidics Corporation Columbia, Md. (4/89-Present).</u>

- Research and development of fluidic devices actuated via air and fluid flow for new product development.
- Responsible for resolving technical problems related to product performance, design and execution of controlled experiments, failure analysis.
- Finite element techniques utilized for analyzing the transient behavior of various turbulent flow fields and heat transfer.
- Responsible for facilitating Design of Experiments Techniques (Taguchi Approach) related to product design and injection molding processes.

<u>Senior Engineer, Dynatherm Corporation Cockeysville, Md. (1/88-4/89).</u>

- Research and development in heat pipe technology and various thermal and mechanical systems related to space and terrestrial applications, for NASA and private industry.
- Component development for spacecraft temperature control, thermal modeling and testing of heat transport systems, heat exchanger design, porous media, fluid flow.
- Experience with both low (refrigerants) and high (liquid metals) temperature applications, stress analysis.

<u>Other Related Positions, West Virginia Tech. (8/85-12/87).</u>

- Research Assistant. Research on heat pipe effective thermal conductivity, start up from frozen state.
- Adjunct Instructor of Mathematics. Taught Analytic Geometry, Pre-Calculus, Algebra, Trigonometry.
- Supervisor and lecturer, Heat & Mass Transfer lab. Conducted experiments in conduction, free/forced convection, radiation, and heat exchangers.

ADDITIONAL SKILLS

Proficient in Basic, Fortran, various word processing software, lotus, macro development, Autocad.

ACTIVITIES

- President/Founder of Graduate Student Organization (G.S.O.) (85-87).
- Student Representative, Graduate Committee (85-87).
- Associate member of ASME

REFERENCES

Available upon request.

Achievements on Each Rung of the Career Ladder

Ready to Take the Next Step

Having proven his abilities, this candidate is ready to move forward into a senior management position at a major industrial products company. This resume, which was selected by the staff of Philadelphia-based Right Associates, follows a fairly strict chronological format, but with some interesting twists.

"This individual's career is notable because it shows unbroken progress in the areas of product management and marketing support," notes a staff member at Right Associates. "Since he has decided to move forward in the same career, a chronological resume takes his best experiences and aims them toward the next level."

Indeed, the Objective section sets that in motion with the statement "Qualified by 15 years of progressive and increasingly responsible positions in industrial and consumer marketing..."

"A prospective employer will recognize a focused professional whose career advancement came from knowledge, initiative and results. The candidate describes his responsibilities from sales analyst through product manager—with an expert's vocabulary," notes a Right staff member.

The headings under each position set off the candidate's responsibilities and the results he achieved. "He shows that with each step up the career ladder he proactively produced measurable and above-average results by implementing, restructuring, negotiating, initiating, designing and developing," notes a member of the Right staff.

"The chronological order strongly supports the concise list of Specific Responsibilities. This list, in turn, frames the candidate for a managerial or maybe even an executive position in sales and/or marketing."

Right Associates

Right Associates, headquartered in Philadelphia, is the world's leading publicly held organization specializing in career management and human resources consulting. The firm has more than 90 offices worldwide. It is well-known for its career transition consulting services, designed to assist employers with termination issues and to help employees develop skills and strategies needed to find new employment.

Name
Address
Phone

OBJECTIVE:
To contribute to the overall success of a progressive, growth-oriented company in a *marketing/sales management position* with diverse responsibilities.

Qualified by fifteen years of progressive and increasingly responsible positions in industrial and consumer marketing, sales and product management with a M.B.A. degree in marketing.

Specific Responsibilities Included:

Strategic Planning	Profit and Loss
Distribution	New Product Development
Market Research	Sales Forecasting
Advertising	Operational Planning

PROFESSIONAL EXPERIENCE

ABC Company, City, State (1976-Present)

Product Manager, Major Product, Major Product Division

RESPONSIBILITIES:

Development and implementation of marketing policies and objective for three major product lines totaling $180,000,000 in sales. Full responsibility for profit, product line strategy, distribution, market share goals, pricing, quality, packaging, margins and the direction of the marketing research and advertising activities related to the product lines. (1982-present)

RESULTS:

- Achieved record sales and earnings for major product line consistently over a two year period with an average compound growth rate of 20% versus an industry average of 8%.
- Restructured product mix through deletion of lower margin items and increasing productivity with sales of higher margin items resulting in optimum product mix and significantly higher product sales.
- Introduced two new product lines within two years and developed new packaging, product improvements and aggressive advertising yielding a 60% increase in market share.
- Implemented new product specifications realizing savings of $250,000 annually.

Marketing Manager, Major Product Division

RESPONSIBILITIES:

Managed direct trade sales, marketing, reciprocal sales agreements and distributed for $350 million division. Marketing efforts focused on business planning, monthly sales forecasting, new product development and capital expansion studies. Sales involved the selling of direct accounts. Supervised the export sales/service function. (1976-1982)

(continued)

Name
Page 2

RESULTS:

- Negotiated and implemented 38 reciprocal sales agreements producing optimum product mix and increased manufacturing productivity while reducing freight costs and yielding $4,000,000 annually in profit.
- Achieved special bonus award for successful marketing of products from new manufacturing facility. Responsibilities and ranking of position increased during tenure to reward performance and expansion of activities.
- Exceeded sales targets each year by more than 10%.

XYZ CORPORATION, INC. City, State (1967-1976)

Marketing Research Analyst, Major Product Division

RESPONSIBILITIES:

Developed business planning, marketing research studies and market evaluations for products in both the industrial and consumer markets for billion dollar division. Supervised market analysts and directed outside consultants. (1973-1976)

RESULTS:

- Designed and directed the initial major marketing study to determine product usage in the residential market.
- Developed computer model to forecast product usage by major end-use market.

Sales Analyst, Major Product Division

RESPONSIBILITIES:

Duties included sales planning and forecasting. Supervised Junior Sales Analyst and Statistical Assistants. (1967-1973)

RESULTS:

Redesigned and implemented unique sales reporting.
Initiated a competitive intelligence system.

EDUCATION:

Master in Business Administration, Marketing, 1982
Name of University—City, State

Bachelor of Science, Marketing, 1974
Name of University—City, State

Name of University Graduate School of Business, 1975
Executive Programs, Marketing and Sales Management

Power Resume Tip

Proofread your resume several times. Remember, if the resume you submit to your prospective employer isn't completely error-free, you might as well kiss the job good-bye.

Remember Your Audience

It's Often What's Up Front That Counts

When the staff at Russell-Rogat Transition Specialists sat down with Mary Williams, they realized they were preparing for a search in one of the tightest fields today—finance. Therefore, they advised the candidate to develop a Career Summary that "showcased" her best qualifications in the first few lines.

The candidate also had to take into account who the likely readers of her resume would be.

"For the finance/accounting area, pointing out Mary's degree, certification and 'nitty-gritty' skills and experience in approximately a half-dozen lines seemed very important," says a representative from the Cleveland-based company. Other features of the resume that are tailored to an audience of finance professionals are the crisp position overviews and accomplishment statement "bullets" pointing to specific contributions.

"The only improvement that might be made to the document," they point out, "is to hone it down further to eliminate some of its bulk. It is still quite a bit of information to sift through."

This could probably be accomplished relatively easily by shortening the position descriptions and limiting the size of the bulleted accomplishments to two lines.

Staff of
Russell-Rogat Transition Specialists, Inc.

Founded in 1984, Russell-Rogat Transition Specialists, Inc., in Cleveland, Ohio, provides corporate-sponsored services in outplacement, career development, work force transition, spouse relocation assistance and pre-retirement planning programs. Through its work, the firm provides customized programs to assist employees managing career change and the resulting transition process. Its motto, "From beginning to beginning," represents the view that the beginning of a change can lead to the beginning of a new opportunity. Russell-Rogat is a member of the Association of Outplacement Consulting Firms.

MARY WILLIAMS

6000 Cherry Hill Drive **Cleveland, Ohio 44000** **Home (216) 555-1111**

OBJECTIVE: Accounting/finance management position with a company seeking experience in budgeting, cost accounting and variance analysis.

CAREER SUMMARY:

- MBA/CPA with ten years financial management reporting including two years public accounting and five years cost accounting.
- Demonstrated experience in project development and installation with mainframe systems, managed staff of five professionals and two support staff.
- Proficient with personal computers. Lotus 1-2-3, dBase and other software packages.
- Able to set and achieve goals, work well independently and under pressure.

EXPERIENCE:

1990 to Present *CLEVELAND HOSPITAL*, Cleveland, Ohio

<u>Fiscal Coordinator, Division of Radiology</u>
Dual report to Administrator of Radiology and Director of Financial Planning. Liaison between Division of Radiology and Finance Division ensuring control over financial issues and corporation policy. Prepared operation budget of $31 million and capital budget of over $7 million. Maintained cost accounting system for Division. Developed cost standards and variance analyses. Assisted with coding and pricing of clinical procedures to ensure maximum reimbursement for services. Prepared various profitability analyses of services and outside ventures.

- Facilitated reorganization of accounting and reporting structure within Division of Radiology to 10 profit centers providing enhanced analysis of percent profit contributed to Division and organization.
- Designed and implemented weekly managerial accounting seminars designed to improve fiscal responsibility of clinical managers by reviewing and teaching techniques to maximize revenue and minimize expenses.
- Developed capital budget monitoring tracking system for justifications and expenditures to ensure most beneficial use of capital funds.

1989 to 1990 *CHANGE SYSTEMS, INC.*, Boston, Massachusetts

<u>Regional Operations Manager</u>
Coordinated installation and after support for mainframe management information/cost accounting system for healthcare institutions. Spearheaded direction and support of regional management team for midwest region. Developed/enhanced implementation and client support procedures. Trained users in both software applications and in flexible budgeting/cost accounting. Developed excellent rapport with clients.

- Recommended changes to installation and after support process reducing length of time to have functioning system and increasing efficiency of resolving problems of clients.
- Established Cleveland office for clients to have greater access to software specialist.

1986 to 1989 — *ST. FRANCIS HOSPITAL*, Cleveland, Ohio

Manager of Cost and Budget
Reported to Director of Financial Planning. Installed and maintained mainframe cost accounting system (Change System Inc.) Prepared operating budget using mainframe budget package. Analyzed and recommended revenue enhancing and cost cutting measures. Assisted with third party contract negotiations and preparation of Medicare Step Down report. Projected various income statements for services within and outside hospital.

- Installed mainframe computer cost accounting system used in analyzing profit and efficiencies of areas within hospital for revenue enhancing and cost cutting measures.
- Organized and taught educational series for non-accountants to improve fiscal responsibility of managers.

1983 to 1986 — *TOWER HOSPITAL*, Cleveland, Ohio

Manager of Financial Reporting
Produced timely financial statements. Prepared operating and capital budget.

- Implemented computerized property accounting system to monitor acquisitions and disposals.
- Computerized many accounting functions, increasing efficiency of accounting department.

1982 to 1983 — *BIG SIX FIRM*, Cleveland, Ohio

Staff Accountant
Responsible for audit tasks and management consulting engagements as part of audit staff. Clients included hospitals, manufacturing, government, not-for-profit agencies and others.

1976 to 1982 — *CASE WESTERN RESERVE UNIVERSITY*, Cleveland, Ohio
Various laboratory/research positions both full and part-time.

EDUCATION:

Case Western Reserve University, Cleveland, Ohio
M.B.A., specialized in Accounting Finance, 1982

Hiram College, Hiram, Ohio
B.A. Biology, 1976

OTHER INFORMATION:

- Certified Public Accountant in Ohio
- Advanced member of Healthcare Financial Management Association
- Board position of Treasurer for Cherry Hill Condominium Association for five years.

Power Resume Tip

Make sure that you are consistent throughout your resume. Be sure to use the same line spacing, headline treatment, listing treatment, etc.

Turning Military Experience Into Work Force Assets

Effective Use of the Functional Style Resume

"Like many other former armed services personnel, Arthur A. Abrams was faced with the challenge of communicating his achievements in the military—where he had spent his entire career—to the civilian job market," observes Samuel J. Sackett, Ph.D. (Sackett is an executive consultant with the Oklahoma office of the executive search firm Bernard Haldane Associates.)

In order to do that effectively, Abrams used a functional format for his resume so that he could emphasize his accomplishments.

"His translation of military accomplishments into the language of the private sector proved ingenious and effective," notes Sackett. The "employees," of course, were soldiers; the "senior executives," general officers; the "heavy construction company" was an engineering battalion; the "foreign entities" were NATO allies; and "upper management" were colonels.

The achievements detailed in Abrams' resume were impressive enough to attract interest.

"This resume worked like a charm," says Sackett. "A prospective employer who had no opening for Major Abrams sent off the resume, unasked, to an executive recruiter who proposed the hiring of the major, again unasked, to a major corporation in quest of an environmental engineer."

Samuel J. Sackett, Ph.D.
Executive Consultant, Bernard Haldane Associates

Samuel J. Sackett, Ph.D., with the Oklahoma City office of Bernard Haldane Associates, came to career counseling after having been a teacher, newspaper reporter, advertising account executive and public relations assignments manager. Dr. Sackett has published articles on job search in the *National Business Employment Weekly*.

ARTHUR A. ABRAMS
1234 Benningham Blvd.
Cabrillo, CA 99401
(456) 789-1000

OBJECTIVE:

A managerial or project manager position that draws on analytical, communications, and problem solving strengths in a growing manufacturing or construction organization.

QUALIFICATIONS:

15 years of experience in management and engineering, including: project team leadership, information management, construction management, and work flow analysis.

ACHIEVEMENTS:

Collected raw data on 500-employee project teams in a 16,000-employee organization on a wide range of management indicators, identified strengths and weaknesses, researched problem areas, briefed senior executives, and recommended improvements which, when implemented, improved organizational efficiency.

Developed improved computer model that reduced cost-tracking errors by 90%.

Developed successful training program for 700-employee heavy construction company, involving exchange of information and joint planning with foreign entities.

Improved complex production plan, including operations, personnel, and logistics, which received commendation by upper management.

Evaluated master planning system which was approved by upper management, coordinated equipment purchases, and trained users.

Scheduled operations, allocated resources, supervised 150-man construction team, and monitored quality on building major concrete and earthwork structures.

Developed and validated pseudocode compiler in BASIC.

Trained engineer company in leadership and communication skills and served as mentor for company commander while assisting in mobilization and deployment for Operation Desert Storm.

EXPERIENCE:

Industrial Engineer
Information Management Office Chief
Automation Specialist
Information Manager
U.S. Army (Civilian Employee)

Engineer Team Leader
Intelligence Officer
U.S. Army Reserve

Company Commander
Platoon Leader
Operations Officer
Training Officer
Supply Officer
Intelligence Officer
Facilities Staff Engineer
U.S. Army

EDUCATION:

MBA - Information Systems
Oklahoma City University

BS - Civil Engineering
Michigan State University

BS - Computer Studies
University of Maryland

PROFESSIONAL AFFILIATIONS:

Registered Professional Engineer
Member, National/Oklahoma Society of Professional Engineers (Chapter Secretary OSPE)
Member, American Society of Civil Engineers

Power Resume Tip

If you're going to print copies of your original resume, *don't* use the copy machine in your office, the library or your local drugstore. These machines are usually not well-maintained. Your best bet is to use a commercial copy shop.

The Value of Good, Clear Writing

The 'Write' Resume Will Stand Out From the Crowd

So few people know how to write well these days that a well-turned phrase in a resume can turn employers' heads.

"Individuals conducting a job search often think of their resume as a simple summary of their professional work history," say Melinda A. Schneider and Richard E. Widuch, partners in Schneider Widuch in Pasadena, California. "However, many employers also use the resume to evaluate a person's communications abilities. A well-written resume always will stand out from the crowd."

Susan O'Shear's resume certainly supports that view. Scanning it, the reader comes away with the impression that the candidate can communicate *clearly*. While one might quibble with some of O'Shear's choices of words, her resume certainly conveys that this candidate "has accomplished specific events each year with important results," say Schneider Widuch.

The consultants point out that the five keys to success in producing effective resumes are "personality, style, content, implementation and impact." The latter three are the areas the candidate must focus on in producing the resume—job responsibilities, what was accomplished in each of those positions and what effects those achievements had.

While doing this, the candidate must also be careful to allow his or her personality to come through. Note at the bottom of the first page of O'Shear's resume, she discusses her management of a downsizing, careful to emphasize that she spent at least 45 minutes with each of the laid-off employees. O'Shear thus portrays herself as a disciplined *and* concerned manager.

"The style should provide a sense of the human being behind the words," say Schneider Widuch. "This approach can cause companies to conclude that you should be hired because the firm will be better off."

Melinda A. Schneider and Richard E. Widuch
Partners, Schneider Widuch

Schneider Widuch, established in 1983, is an outplacement firm dedicated to assisting management and individuals achieve their business and career goals. The firm is particularly successful with those individuals having strong personalities and those who need sensitive, caring guidance and confidence enhancement. Each participant's program is uniquely developed and delivered based on the personal and career needs of the individual. The firm does not use any type of "canned" outplacement program. Schneider Widuch is a member of the Association of Outplacement Consulting Firms International (AOCFI).

SUSAN A. O'SHEAR
925 Palm Drive
Glendale, California 91202
Telephone: (818) 555-1992

SUMMARY

A successful cross-industry experienced Senior Human Resources professional with a proven track record in dynamic business environments.

SELECTED ACHIEVEMENTS

- Managed the merger integration process in Los Angeles on behalf of Bank of America Corporate Services Group located in San Francisco and Security Pacific Corporation through intensive one-on-one meetings with affected employees explaining rights, options, and all aspects of the Merger Transition Program during a two month period.

- Managed the elimination of the Corporate Aviation Department, including business case development and analysis, employee separations and the transfer of operations to alternative service providers, which saved the Corporation more than $2.6 million.

- Managed the staffing strategy for the Gibraltar acquisition to ensure that key employees were retained during the conversion of treasury and finance operations.

- Designed and implemented with executive management a performance evaluation system targeted towards corporate financial managers and professional staff.

- Created a "Mentor Program" for minority corporate officers. The program was implemented under the direction of the Multi-Cultural Officers Network organization.

PROFESSIONAL EXPERIENCE

BANK OF AMERICA, Los Angeles, CA — 1992

Vice President, Manager, Merger Integration — Los Angeles, Executive Staff

Reported to Vice President, Corporate Services Group. Responsible for managing the merger integration process between Security Pacific Corporation and Bank of America. The process involved intensive meetings and discussions with affected employees; planning and implementation of strategies to retain essential staff and to reduce staff where necessary to ensure the profitability goals of the merger. Directly eliminated 211 employees through intensive one-on-one meetings with each meeting lasting between 45 minutes to several hours during the 60 day period. Developed the Senior Vice President and above displacement plan and was responsible for unit close down and securing assets.

SECURITY PACIFIC CORPORATION, Los Angeles, CA 1983 — 1992

Vice President, Senior Human Resources Consultant, 1986 — 1992

Reported to Senior Vice President, Human Resources Services, and served a client base of over 800 executives, managers and professionals. Responsibilities included Employee Relations with accountability for implementing, communicating and interpreting policies, programs and legal issues, resolution of grievances, and reduction-in-force business case implementation; Employment and Management Recruiting with accountability for development and execution of recruiting strategies, staffing and organizational analysis and career transition counseling; Management Development with accountability for assessing developmental needs and providing programs to increase professional growth and maximize productivity; and Compensation with responsibility for developing job evaluations, job family descriptions, career path models and succession plans in support of retention strategy and expense control targets.

Vice President, Manager, Management Development 1983 — 1986

Reported to Senior Vice President, Human Resources. Directly responsible for a Division that provided supervisory and management skills training to the Corporation. Managed the Educational Assistance, Career Management and New Employee Orientation programs. Annual operating budget of $2.1 million and 14 professional training staff members. Previous assignments were Manager, Training Operations and Senior Program Designer.

TECHNICOLOR, INC., Los Angeles, CA 1982 — 1983

National Training Director

Reported to Vice President, Operations. Responsible for the creation and startup of the training function for a new subsidiary. Created "Technicolor Tech", a multi-week training program encompassing personnel policy and administration, financial management, sales and customer service training and technical areas. Wrote and published company operating manual with line management.

ORANGE JULIUS OF AMERICA, Santa Monica, CA 1978 — 1982

National Training Director

Reported to Vice President, Operations. Responsible for the creation of "Orange Julius University", an intensive business management training program for new franchisees. Previous assignments were Western Regional Training Manager and National Communications Director.

EDUCATION

UCLA, Los Angeles, CA, B.A. Degree

Continuing education: Advanced Program for Human Resources Executives, University of Michigan; Advanced Conference on Labor Relations Law, IAML; Organizational Consulting Program, Skopos.

RELATED ACTIVITIES

Personnel Policy Committee, San Fernando Valley Girl Scout Council.
Society for Human Resource Management.
Adviser, Multi-Cultural Officers Network, Security Pacific Corporation.
Founding Member, Security Pacific's SpeakersBank, a volunteer organization providing public speakers to professional and nonprofit community organizations.

Power Resume Tip

Leave at least one inch at the top of the page, and use one-inch margins around the other three borders as well. Never go smaller than a half-inch margin. Large margins create a pleasing, organized, uncluttered feeling and many employers use that space to make notes.

A Resume With Personality

This Candidate Went Out On a Limb Without Falling

"This resume defies convention in several ways," says Penny Shaw, executive vice president of Lee Hecht Harrison, one of the nation's largest and most well-known outplacement firms.

"Although the writer has at least 26 years of experience, he has covered everything in one page. That's certainly not the norm, but it is very important for someone in the advertising business who communicates with words!"

Shaw also notes that George Smith's resume is unusual because of the many things it *doesn't* have. Notice that Smith omitted dates of employment and a job objective. "By not using dates," notes Shaw, "the writer has lessened the possible temptation for the resume reviewer to judge him first by his age. And by not including a job objective, the candidate keeps the door wide open for opportunities on either the agency or client side of the business."

Also notice that the candidate has shunned the usual "resume speak"—incomplete sentences, phrases beginning with action words—in favor of a "story" in the first person. The result is that this document sound less like a resume than it does a conversation with a person you meet at a party.

"This resume has personality," emphasizes Shaw. "From the 12-word summary statement at the top—which tells the reader succinctly what the writer is all about—to the organization of the document, to the breezy yet highly professional style, the resume works!"

Penny Shaw
Executive Vice President, Lee Hecht Harrison

Lee Hecht Harrison is one of the nation's premier outplacement and career management firms, with offices located throughout the United States. Founded in 1974, the company helps organizations and their employees deal with today's complex and challenging career transition issues.

George L. Smith

531 Church Street
New York, NY 10044

Office: 212-555-2000
Home: 212-555-6180

A major advertising agency account executive who used to be a client.

MY BACKGROUND

Ad Agency DDB Needham. Account Supervisor in this agency and its great predecessor, Doyle Dane Bernbach, for over 12 years. The account is GTE. Primarily, I have worked in the corporate account areas. Additionally, I have handled GTE defense systems, precious metals, electrical and electronic equipment and commercial/industrial lighting.

In a nutshell, it's my job to draw out pertinent marketing/product/service information and relay it to appropriate people in the agency. Then, to represent the agency in presenting the resulting work to the client.

I've worked with all media including network TV, business and consumer magazines, outdoor, radio and newspapers. And, of course, I work on a daily basis with clients, agency management, creatives and media representatives.

Client Sylvania Electrical Products. For 14 years, I was with this major electronics corporation. I worked in all areas of sales promotion, advertising and other activities, serving several divisions as Ad Manager and/or Marketing Services Manager. I had to interface effectively with company management, suppliers, distributors, retailers and the advertising agency.

ABOUT ME

St. Johns University and Queens College—Marketing.

Willing to relocate (though I love New York, too).

Excellent health, married.

Make Your Resume *Work*

Eliminate Clutter and Confusion

"I like this resume because it is results oriented," says Vicki Spina, who heads her own career consulting service in Chicago. "Stevens has made effective use of white space and boldfaced heads. The type is clean and very readable."

Also, Spina says, the summary is interesting. "It draws the reader in," she adds. "In addition, there is good use of action words."

Stevens's resume, reprinted from Spina's book, *Getting Hired in the '90s*, covers a number of years and several jobs, yet the information is organized in such a neat, almost understated way to insure that there is no clutter or confusion.

Vicki Spina
Corporate Image

Vicki Spina is the owner of Corporate Image, a career consulting service in Schaumburg, Illinois. She is the author of *Getting Hired in the '90s*. Spina presents seminars based on her book. She also serves as a consultant, speaker and teacher. Spina is often featured as a career strategist on CNBC television and is frequently quoted on career matters in print and electronic media around the country.

Samuel Stevens
519 Hartland Avenue
Bartlett, IL 60103 (708) 724-8367

SUMMARY/HIGHLIGHTS

Proactive team administrator with a proven track record in Human Resources and Marketing

Implemented corrective action plan resulting in retention of a $1,000,000 national account.
Streamlined personnel staff saving $50,000 in employee compensation annually.
Orchestrated most successful United Way Campaign in company history.
Reduced operating expenses by 20% (annual savings of over $100,000).

EDUCATION

Bachelor of Science Degree/Marketing
University of Wisconsin–1977
Professional Human Resource Certification Program–1993

PROFESSIONAL HISTORY

XYZ Management Group 7/92 to 8/93
Business Development Consultant

Project manager for successful recruitment selection campaigns with Fortune 500 Companies including: M/M Mars, Sears, Advo Systems Inc.

- Rebuilt a faltering facilities staffing program through effective management of human resources, daily operations and client servicing.

Risk Insurers Inc. 6/86 to 7/92
Regional Personnel Manager (400 employees)

Effectively managed a staff of 25 for a 10-office region with P/L of $1,000,000.

- Designed and implemented a flexible benefits plan which improved insurance coverage and saved company $5,000 in annual premiums.
- Established an effective college recruitment program which attracted top-quality employees and enhanced overall company productivity.
- Developed and conducted innovative training programs resulting in improved employee/manager morale and reduction of turnover by 20%.

Family Group Insurance 5/83 to 6/86
Branch Personnel/Office Manager (100 employees)

Autonomy for re-organizing staffing and employee relation programs. Instrumental in creating a team environment and establishing effective communication channels.

- Initiated employee discussion groups which identified productivity problems. Recommended appropriate solutions to management which were implemented, resulting in improved employee relations and company profitability.
- Recruited and hired an additional 20% staff in 90-day period.

Echo Shoe Manufacturing Company 1/80 to 5/83
Personnel Manager

Organized a start-up personnel department for 75 non-union staff employees. Coordinated activities of payroll, accounting and support services to insure smooth operations.

ABC Department Stores 9/77 to 1/80
Personnel Manager

- Rapidly promoted from Executive Trainee to Assistant Buyer to Employment Interviewer and Personnel Manager in less than three years.

COMMUNITY ACTIVITIES

Active Member/Society for Human Resource Management, 1987 to present
International Foundation of Employee Benefit Plans
Elected Chairman United Way Effectiveness Council, 1991-1992

ADDITIONAL TRAINING/SKILLS

Computer literate on PC-based Human Resource Programs
Work Force Diversity 2000
Employment Law in Illinois

Power Resume Tip

Avoid including personal statistics, hobbies or outside interests on your resume. This information is usually irrelevant and may even bias a potential employer against you.

Functional *and* Effective

You Can Have It Both Ways

"A functional resume *can* be effective," says Beth Stefani, owner of Resumes, Etc. in Hamburg, New York.

"This resume helped Mr. Winslow secure an interview with a prestigious securities investment firm," she adds. "He's currently working there as the pension accounts sales manager and first vice president of investments."

Winslow had spent 20 years in commercial banking at four different banks in western New York. He was ready for a change. "His resume reflects a change of direction, from banking to business development/sales and business consulting," Stefani says.

"The directional arrows highlight the various categories and add a bold, eye-catching appearance to his resume. It is professional, yet dramatic at the same time."

After the reader has reviewed Winslow's strengths and achievements, his employment history and other pertinent information can be found on the second page. And, with the clean, direct and appealing look of the resume, readers are sure to turn to the second page—and keep reading.

Beth W. Stefani, Ed.M., MBA
Owner/Consultant, Resumes, Etc.

Resumes, Etc., located in Hamburg, New York, specializes in custom-designed resumes and cover letters, career counseling and job search advisement. In addition to providing individual assistance to job hunters on a personal referral basis, Stefani provides outside consulting to RW Caldwell Associates, Inc., an outplacement consulting firm in Williamsville, New York. Previously, she worked in commercial lending and corporate credit analysis at Chase Manhattan Bank and Marine Midland Bank in Buffalo, New York. Earlier, as a career counselor at the State University of New York at Buffalo, Stefani managed the campus recruitment program for business and engineering graduates.

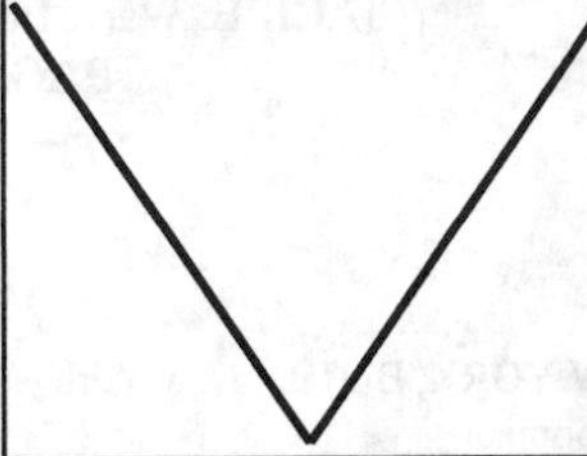

JACK E. WINSLOW

33 Dawn Drive, Hamburg, New York 14075
Residence: (716) 555-5555
Office: (716) 555-5555

SUMMARY OF QUALIFICATIONS

An experienced professional in all phases of business including sales, marketing, financial analysis, administration, and management. Skilled in written and verbal communication, business development, negotiating and closing sales, and ongoing relationship management.

BUSINESS DEVELOPMENT/SALES

Sold financial services products to the medical community and small to medium sized businesses within the service and manufacturing industries. Provided financial services to professional groups including attorneys, accountants and physicians.

Developed customer base through referrals of current customers, solicitation of accountants and attorneys, and an active cold calling program.

Produced the second highest gross volume of financial services products for the first quarter of 1994, after having ranked fourth out of fourteen sales representatives in 1993, statewide.

While working for a limited network branch bank, achieved 120% of loan goal, exceeded deposit goal by 200%, and exceeded prospecting goal by 150%.

Spearheaded the development of a new lending program for minority business owners through the New York State Urban Development Corp. Personally closed 75% of all loans generated during the first two years of the program.

BUSINESS CONSULTING

Provided individual consulting to small businesses regarding capital expenditures, expansion, product mix, marketing techniques and other business decisions.

Developed thorough knowledge of customers' businesses, including production, marketing and sales, credit management, financial structuring, and other aspects.

FINANCIAL ANALYSIS

Analyzed financial statements to assess financial stability, turnover of assets and cash flow needs. Determined financing and loan structuring appropriate to business needs.

RELATIONSHIP BUILDING/MANAGEMENT

Emphasized long-term continuing business relationships with all customers. This was accomplished through broad-based understanding of and ready responsiveness to customer needs.

EMPLOYMENT HISTORY

1992 - 1994 EQUITY GOLD BANK OF NEW YORK, Buffalo, New York
Vice President of Business Development

1989 - 1992 BANKING TRUST COMPANY, Buffalo, New York
Assistant Vice President and Commercial Loan Officer

1986 - 1989 WASHINGTON FIRST BANK, Buffalo, New York
Assistant Vice President and Northeast District Loan Officer
Manager of Custom Financial Center

1974 - 1986 MARINER TRUST, Buffalo, New York
Assistant Vice President and Commercial Loan Officer
Senior Credit Analyst, Branch Bank Manager

EDUCATION AND MILITARY SERVICE

M.B.A., Finance, 1977
State University of New York at Buffalo, New York

B.A., Economics, 1971
Syracuse University, Syracuse, New York

Second Lieutenant, U.S. Army - Adjutant General Corps, 1972-1974

CONTINUING EDUCATION

Sales and Marketing (3-week Seminar), 1992
Action Systems, Rochester, New York

Group Presentation Skills Seminar, 1990
Banking Trust Company, Buffalo, New York

Commercial Lending (3-week Seminar), 1983
School of Management, State University of New York at Buffalo

Credit Analysis (6-week Seminar), 1980
Mariner Trust, Buffalo, New York

COMMUNITY INVOLVEMENT

Vice President of Foundation Board, Children's Hospital, Buffalo, NY 1990-Present
President (1983-84), Current Member, Kiwanis Club of Hamburg, NY
Treasurer and Manager, Hamburg Girl's Softball League, 1987-Present
Civic Affairs Chairman (1992-93), Current Member, Rotary Club of Hamburg

Power Resume Tip

Include information about your high school education only if you are a recent graduate or did not attend college or a trade school—in other words, if it is the most important educational credential you have.

'Downsized' Out of Job May Mean 'Downsizing' Resume

Even the Highly Experienced Can Have One-Page Resumes

When his subsidiary was divested, Jon Dow, a 30-year veteran of the work force, suddenly found himself out of a job. Candidates with this much experience often write three- or four-page resumes, reports Swain & Swain Inc. founder Robert Swain. However, his Jon Dow knew that in this tough employment climate it's best to make your resume easily readable.

"An easy scan of this resume should tell the reader just enough to decide whether the experience and credentials are appropriate for a prospective opening," says Swain, the co-author of *Out the Organization*. "The task of presenting a long record of experience runs headlong into the limited attention span of resume readers. In fact, we doubt that resumes are ever *read*—believing that most are merely scanned."

Particularly strong is the Background Summary, which provides two concise sentences and six points making the candidate's areas of expertise stand out clearly.

This resume shoots down the claim of so many candidates that they "can't fit everything" onto one page.

Robert Swain
Founder, Swain & Swain Inc.

Robert Swain is founder and chairman of Swain & Swain Inc., a corporate outplacement firm in New York and Connecticut, specializing in senior management assignments. Swain is co-author of *Out the Organization*, now in its third printing by Master Media.

JON DOW
596 Overlook Avenue
New York, NY 10031
212-555-6543

BACKGROUND SUMMARY

GENERAL MANAGER with extensive experience in marketing and sales, operations, R&D, and the financial management of medium and high-tech businesses. Product knowledge spans lasers & optronics, telecommunications, energy, industrial products and computer services. Related areas of expertise are:

Market Development	Quality Control	Productivity Improvement
Product Engineering	Turnarounds	Cost Reduction Programs

EXPERIENCE

JONES/LOCKWOOD (formerly Lockwood Co.)
President, Garden City, N.Y., since 1989.
Manage this profitable $12 million subsidiary in the development, manufacturing and sale of scientific equipment to the aerospace, industrial, university, OEM, defense and export markets. Responsible for U.S. and Canadian sales and operations, R&D, finance and human resources. During last two years, sales have increased 20% in a depressed market, while profits rose from a loss of $1.5 million to a positive contribution of $1 million. Significantly upgraded engineering and office support computer systems and software. Company recently acquired from French parent by Jones Corporation, a U.S. company.

XYZ CORPORATION.
Director, North American Marketing & Sales, XYZ Belgium, 1983 to 1988
Based in New Jersey, developed and directed North American sales office, achieving substantial growth in the export distribution of sophisticated electronic control devices. Built solid customer base, contributed 50% of company's total income, and expanded established product lines with new technologies.

Director, Operations, XYZ Belgium, 1979 to 1983
Based in the Hague with P&L and turnaround responsibility for 950 employees, multi-plant operations, producing telecommunications equipment and military electronics. Achieved profitable status through implementation of: cost reduction program; on-line computer design capability; and 50% increase in factory efficiency. Unit went from $2 million annual loss to net profit of $1.5 million.

Director, Operations, XYZ Scandinavia, 1977 to 1979.
Based in Copenhagen with responsibility for operations of 5 companies with sales of +$500 million. Planned and implemented expansion programs in two countries, consolidated two manufacturing operations and established highly profitable co-production facility for F-16 electronics.

Operations Executive, XYZ World Headquarters, New York, 1972 to 1977.
Developed and implemented major improvement programs at various XYZ companies worldwide, spanning telecommunications, automotive, industrial and consumer goods.

Earlier XYZ assignments included establishing new company to manufacture submarine cables and serving as assistant to Vice President, Operations, focusing on cost improvement and return on assets, 1962 to 1972.

EDUCATION

B.S.I.E., College of Mechanical Technology, Brussels.

PERSONAL

Married, two children. Multi-lingual (English, Dutch, German, French).

No Unnecessary Baggage

A Resume That Hits the Target

"Although there are many types of resumes from one page to 30 pages," says John J. Turnblacer, "I like this one because it is very simple, to the point, easy to follow and easy to read. All of the pertinent information is contained within this simple format, and superfluous words, such as 'references available upon request,' are excluded. In addition to being well-drafted, the resume is easy on the reader's eye."

Turnblacer is president of Executive Assets. He likes this jam-packed resume because "when you first look at it, you know exactly what the individual is—a sales and marketing executive."

He also notes that within the Professional Experience section, the companies and positions are very readable upon a quick scan.

"Achievements are well-highlighted with quantification, but not puffed out of proportion. The Education and Professional Training sections are presented in a straightforward manner, even though the candidate has no degree."

The candidate delivers a concise summary of accomplishments under the heading for each employer mentioned. These paragraphs are followed by an impressive list of succinctly stated achievements.

John J. Turnblacer
President, Executive Assets

John J. Turnblacer is based in Philadelphia with overall responsibility for this high-quality performance management consulting firm. He counsels top executives through the job-campaign process and advises client companies in planning staff changes.

Prior to joining Executive Assets, he held executive-level positions for ITT, Citicorp and Allied Signal, in operations, human resources and administration with global responsibilities.

Turnblacer is a member of the Society for Human Resource Management and has been a member of several state bars. He holds a J.D. degree from Chase College of Law and a B.S. from the University of Dayton.

JOHN HENRY

275385 South Ardmore Road (h) 215-555-1234
Villanova, PA 19073 (o) 215-555-5678

SALES/MARKETING EXECUTIVE

Over twenty-five years of top management experience in the domestic and international automobile, truck and construction equipment industries with extensive background in marketing, dealer development, and sales initiatives. Successful record of building national field organizations in parts and service as well as vehicle sales. Skilled in the preparation of operating plans and development of budgets and pricing analyses. A dynamic success-oriented manager who demands and gets the most from subordinates. Outstanding verbal and written communications skills.

PROFESSIONAL EXPERIENCE

JI CASE COMPANY Racine, WI 1991-1992
Division of Tenneco. Manufacturer of construction equipment; world-wide sales of $3.6 billion.

Regional Manager
Northeast US/Eastern Canada
Managed staff of 12, 90 dealers, responsible for marketing, dealer development, customer satisfaction, sales of $180 million.

- Reduced region inventory from $50 million to less than $3 million by utilizing selldown promotions and dealer incentives.
- Increased market share in an industry which was in a decline of 35-40%.
- Implemented procedures to promote customer service/satisfaction including assigning an individual at each dealership, utilizing customer surveys, encouraging district managers to follow-up on key accounts.
- Attained an "under budget" condition by initiating cost cuts in areas which did not affect sales or service.

SUBARU OF AMERICA Cherry Hill, NJ 1988-1991

Director - Market Development
Developed, coordinated and implemented national policies and procedures for the business management, dealer development and market planning departments. Objectives included increasing sales per outlet and enhancing the value of the franchise through upgrading existing dealers and appointing qualified new dealers in open points.

- Improved sales per outlet by designing and following "Blue print" for upgrading dealer performance. Tracked monthly, replaced dealers where performance was poor.
- Co-chaired committee for hiring and training entry level management trainees. Success of program led to 10 new Field District Sales Managers in 2 years.
- Developed and published Subaru Market Development Policy Manual containing national policies and procedures regarding franchise and representation issues. Approved by legal staff and top management. Remains in effect today.
- Created a confidential product book for new dealer solicitation.
- Developed regional marketing plans for the Midwest and California.

AMERICAN MOTORS CORPORATION Southfield, MI 1972-1988

Director - Field Sales Operations (1985-1988)
Directed a staff of 15 and a national field organization of 340: headquartered in 8 regional offices; serviced 1500 dealers; sales objectives 350,000 units and $3 billion annually.

- Improved productivity of field sales organization by over 50%.
- Attained all time monthly sales record of over 23,000 Jeep vehicles.
- Reduced plant inventory of 10,000 units in 2 months with "0% APR" incentive.
- Reviewed and approved all dealer co-op advertising with $15 million budget.

Director - Sales - Central/Southfield, MI (1982-1985)
- West/Denver, CO

Directed and supervised 200 personnel in 4 zones to accomplish sales, parts and service objectives for over 500 dealers. Chaired the California Marketing Committee responsible for developing and executing a special advertising and merchandising budget of $5 million.

- Coordinated the site selection and construction of three company-owned dealerships.
- Completed a successful launch of the Renault Alliance-1983 Motor Trend Car of the Year and Jeep Cherokee-1984 4x4 of the Year.
- Improved market share of Jeep in California.

Director - Jeep Marketing Southfield, MI (1981-1982)
Responsible for marketing, planning, advertising, sales promotion, product information and production control functions for Jeep vehicles in a brand manager marketing concept. Controlled a $40 million budget. Directed a staff of 12 and interfaced with Compton Advertising, sales and manufacturing personnel to develop monthly production controls.

- Increased sales of Jeep CJ by 45%.
- Designed and implemented a direct mail program for Jeep Grand Wagoneer which increased sales by 10%.
- Designed the launch of the XJ (Cherokee) Project.
- Developed the "Why buy a car when you can drive a Jeep" advertising campaign.

Director - Sales Operations Southfield, MI (1981)
Directed and supervised National Vehicle Distribution, Market Representation, Business Management and Dealer Relations Departments consisting of 54 personnel located in 3 plant locations and central office.

- Approved all dealer franchising actions including buy/sells, open points, terminations.
- Coordinated and integrated computer systems network between AMC and Renault in France for vehicle distribution.
- Managed the national dealer council and coordinated the annual meeting process.

Zone Manager Multiple AMC sites (1972-1980)

EDUCATION

Business Management Certificate *Northwood Institute*
Attending The Wharton School *University of Pennsylvania*
BBA Program Business Administration with a focus on Marketing

PROFESSIONAL TRAINING

Kepner, Tregoe--Executive Decision Program
Chrysler Corporation Quality Improvement Program (QIP)
Subaru Leadership Development Seminar
Training in TV and Radio Interview Techniques

MILITARY

US Navy Reserve 1959-1961
2nd Class Petty Officer, Destroyer duty, Pacific Fleet

Power Resume Tip

Select white, off-white, ivory or buff-colored paper for your resume. These colors not only ensure easier readability, they're the least likely to inflame personal bias. You should also select a good-quality, medium-weight paper.

The Solution to an Employer's Problems

This Resume Eliminates the Negative

This resume is noteworthy because what is left *out* is just as important as what this successful candidate chose to include.

Notes Craig VanKouwenberg of The Shelbourne Group, Ltd., an outplacement and career development firm in Lancaster, Pennsylvania, "This resume format was selected to avoid emphasizing those items that might be detractors in today's job market."

VanKouwenberg points out that this resume does not emphasize the candidate's age, although it provides enough information so that it can be quickly estimated.

"All effective resumes will suggest how the candidate might be a solution to an employer's problems," stresses VanKouwenberg. He notes that this resume is an effective "discussion starter," providing a quick scan of Thomas Beardly's progression through the job ranks, allowing the candidate's most desirable qualities (leadership, financial knowledge, management skills) to shine through and filling only one page.

"This candidate had the background to justify two short, high-power statements of accomplishment. And they are two that imply that the candidate easily could have provided many more."

VanKouwenberg explains why the candidate did not use a job objective. "The resume was always delivered in person or accompanied by a highly personalized letter that provided both focus and job objective for the reader. This personalization is the most important key in every effective job search."

Why doesn't this candidate call greater attention to the fact that he is blessed with 20 years of solid on-the-job experience? "Well, that number can be deduced," says VanKouwenberg, "but since most of that experience came with one employer, we didn't want to do too much to suggest that this was someone too old to be flexible and productive."

Indeed, sometimes less *is* more.

Craig VanKouwenberg
The Shelbourne Group, Ltd.

Craig L. VanKouwenberg began his formal work in the employment field as an army chaplain during the Vietnam era. He designed and developed the first (Pennsylvania) state-approved training program in outplacement and career development techniques. A pioneer in the uses of video for career development, he has served as a resource consultant for Joyce Lain Kennedy's national "Careers" column, for psychologists and other professionals working in the employment services industry, and for government and university employment transition programs. He is a Certified Career Development Consultant who accomplished his doctoral studies at Princeton Theological Seminary.

Thomas A. Beardly

1234 Hilltown Road
Yorktown, PA 14151

Evenings: (717) 555-9889
Days: (717) 555-8765

AREAS OF SPECIAL EXPERTISE

Management and Analysis
for
Operations and Finance

Leadership ... Team Building ... Communications

Offer both profit and people orientation to maximize efficiencies, productivity and profitability— while building a strong work force.

PROFESSIONAL HISTORY

1973- Present — Fortune 100 Company, New City, PA and Faraway City, PA
Promoted from Staff Accountant to Controller to Operations Manager

1972-73 — County Hospital/Long-Term Care Facility, Hometown, PA
Accountant

1971-72 — Wholesale Distributor, Hometown, PA
Accountant

SELECTED ACCOMPLISHMENTS

Maintained profitability at 25% above industry norms during declining market and recession.

Changed adversary relationships between union and management to cooperative relationships.

EDUCATION

1971- Present — More than 500 class hours in Management, Finance, GAAP, OSHA, EAP, Personnel, Personnel Supervision

1971 — Indiana University of Pennsylvania
Indiana, PA
B.S. in Business Administration

EXCELLENT REFERENCES AVAILABLE

Lights, Camera, Action (Verbs)!

Exciting the Potential Employer

"This resume emphasizes what the individual can do for the company, not what the company can do for the individual," according to Sharon Worlton and Sally Morrison of LDS Employment in Naperville, Illinois. "That's one of the reasons it is one of our favorites."

Other reasons high on Worlton and Morrison's list include:

- It is clean with lots of white space.
- It uses short, concise statements, making it easy to read quickly.
- It begins selling the individual in the very first sentence and then it *sells, sells, sells*.
- It focuses on achievements using specific numbers, percents and money.
- It uses action verbs to start off each accomplishment.
- If the double lines were eliminated at the top, it would be computer scannable.
- It uses key words that a human resources person would be seeking.
- Overall impression: professional, brief and capable.

Sharon Worlton and Sally Morrison
LDS Employment

Sharon Worlton and Sally Morrison are employees of LDS Employment, a nonprofit organization supported by the Church of Jesus Christ of Latter-Day Saints. They work with individuals from a very wide range of professions (from general labor to CEOs). Their program provides job search training, job and network referrals, career counseling, resume assistance and a job seeker's resource center with telephones, fax service, typewriters and computers. All services are free. Sharon has worked for LDS Employment for 10 years, and Sally has worked there for seven. Sharon just completed serving as past president of the National Association for Job Search Training.

NANCY L. CRENSHAW
000 West Hollywood
Los Angeles, California 90022
(111) 992-0001 Home
(111) 886-1236 Messages

Experienced human resource professional with strong interpersonal, communication and organizational skills. Achievement recognized in the design and implementation of innovative, cost-effective programs in communications, benefits and employee relations.

EXPERIENCE

Armour Dial Corporation, Downers Grove, IL., 1989 to Present

Benefit Analyst

- **Restyled company-wide newsletter to a more positive employee-oriented communication tool. 1991 cost for bi-monthly publication for 12,000 employees was $ 52,000.00.**
- **Authored 90% of all employee and ERISA-mandated communications and reports such as summary-plan descriptions, employee handbook and revisions, and 5,500 filings and summary-annual reports.**
- **Restructured corporate short-term disability program to incorporate third-party medical review. Savings for first year were $50,000.**
- **Designed and installed a direct certification system with insurance carriers. System eliminated extension of benefits to ineligibles.**

McDonald's Corporation, Oak Brook, IL., 1977 to 1989

Benefit Analyst, 1984-1989

- **Spearheaded contagious disease task force to control in-store instances of infectious disease; instrumental in preventing store shutdowns.**
- **Acted as trouble-shooter on short-term and long-term disability claims, sought medical review where necessary and resolved claim disputes.**
- **Responsible for indemnity and HMO plan administration including communications and enrollment for 15,000 employees nationwide.**
- **Monitored flexible-spending account, pre-tax dependent care program for Company: ensured success for maintenance of program. Proposed elimination due to administration expense and low employee participation.**

Relocation Specialist, 1977-1984

- **Managed all phases of in-house executive relocation program. This entailed appraisal process, equity advances, final-closing documentation and home inventory negotiations. Relocated 220 executives per year.**

EDUCATION & DESIGNATIONS

City College. 3.67 GPA (9 courses remaining for BA, English)
Chairman, New England Village Homeowner Association

Index